"What a compassionate and enlightened book! It guides the retreatant through all the difficulties and pitfalls on the path."

RABBI ZALMAN M. SCHACHTER-SHALOMI
P'nai Or Religious Fellowship

"In his second exciting book, David Cooper speaks to contemporary readers in a language more accessible than traditional texts on meditation and spirituality. He helps seekers avoid spiritual cul-de-sacs by weaving psychological issues into the context of meditation."

PIR VILAYAT INAYAT KHAN
Sufi Order

"Drawing on his many years of inner experience, David Cooper clearly and skillfully articulates the essence of the wisdom traditions in a way that makes practical sense."

TARA BENNETT-GOLEMAN, M.A.
psychotherapist and meditation teacher

# THE HEART
# OF
# STILLNESS

*The Elements of*
*Spiritual Practice*

DAVID A. COOPER

BELL TOWER
NEW YORK

Grateful acknowledgment is made to the following for permission to reprint: Doubleday, a division of Bantam Doubleday Dell Publishing Group Inc., for excerpts from *The Three Pillars of Zen* by Philip Kapleau. Copyright © 1965 by Philip Kapleau, copyright © 1980 by the Zen Center, Inc.; Feldheim Publishers Ltd. for excerpts from *The Way of God* by Moshe Chayim Luzzatto, translated by Aryeh Kaplan. Copyright © 1983 by Feldheim Publishers Ltd; Koren Publishers Jerusalem Ltd., Jerusalem, Israel, for excerpts from *The Jerusalem Bible*. Copyright © 1984 by Koren Publishers Jerusalem, Ltd.; Paulist Press for excerpts from *Abraham Isaac Kook*, Ben Zion Bokser, translator. Copyright © 1978 by Ben Zion Bokser, and from *Teresa of Avila: The Interior Castle*, Kieran Kavanaugh, O.C.D., and Otilio Rodriguez O.C.D., translators. Copyright © 1979 by the Washington Province of Discalced Carmelites, Inc.; Penguin Books Ltd. for excerpts from *Be As You Are: The Teachings of Sri Ramana Maharshi*, edited by David Godman (Arkana, 1985). Copyright © 1985 by Sri Ramana Maharshi; Self-Realization Fellowship for excerpts from *Autobiography of a Yogi* by Paramahansa Yogananda. Copyright © 1946 by Paramahansa Yogananda, renewed 1974 by Self-Realization Fellowship. Copyright © 1981 by Self-Realization Fellowship; Charles E. Tuttle Co., Inc., for excerpts from *Zen Flesh, Zen Bones* by Paul Reps. Copyright © 1957 by Charles E. Tuttle Co., Inc.; the University of North Carolina Press for excerpts from *Mystical Dimensions of Islam* by Annemarie Schimmel. Copyright © 1978 by the University of North Carolina Press; Samuel Weiser, Inc., for excerpts from *Meditation and Kabbalah* by Aryeh Kaplan. Copyright © 1982 by Aryeh Kaplan.

Published by Bell Tower, an imprint of Harmony Books,
a division of Crown Publishers, Inc.
201 East 50th Street, New York, New York 10022.
Member of the Crown Publishing Group.

Random House, Inc. New York, Toronto,
London, Sydney, Auckland.
Originally published in hardcover by Bell Tower in 1992.
Bell Tower and colophon are trademarks of
Crown Publishers, Inc.
Manufactured in the United States of America
Book design by Debbie Glasserman

Library of Congress Cataloging-in-Publication Data

Cooper, David A., 1939–
The heart of stillness: the elements of spiritual practice /
David A. Cooper.—1st ed.
p.    cm.
Includes bibliographical references and index.
1. Spiritual life. 2. Spiritual exercises. I. Title.
BL624.C664    1992
291.4′48—dc20    92-4
CIP

ISBN 0-517-88187-X
10  9  8  7  6  5  4  3  2  1
First Paperback Edition

# CONTENTS

CONTENTS

# PREFACE

Human inquiry into the nature of the mind has been a consistent theme since the beginning of history. From the moment of the first "Aha!"—when someone realized there was a thinker behind a personal thought—we have probed and scrutinized our internal process in an effort to understand how it works. The basis of this search, I believe, is our intuition that a momentous secret of creation will be revealed when we finally comprehend the origin of thought.

Although science has significantly multiplied our base of knowledge during the twentieth century, little has been added to the wisdom of thousands of years regarding the function of the mind and the inception of thought. Clearly, science has opened new avenues of inquiry; it has developed tools of measurement and methods of evaluation. Yet, the central effort of self-inquiry is personal, better accomplished by individuals working in silence and solitude than in laboratory or academic situations.

A great deal of today's knowledge is difficult to acquire. We must engage many years in specific fields of inquiry to gain a working framework, and even then our endeavor may be limited to a single limb on a tree of knowledge that includes hundreds of other branches of study. Thus, most human intellectual achievement is inaccessible to the average person except on the most cursory level.

The opposite is true of self-inquiry. Each of us has the potential to dwell in realms of understanding of the highest order; each of us may achieve the qualities of personal development that were realized by the greatest masters known to humankind. This does not necessitate learning great volumes of information, or does it require special intellectual aptitude. Admission to the school of self-inquiry is dependent rather on our motivation, willingness, and effort to explore the inner dimension of our own being.

*The Heart of Stillness* is a primer for this kind of investigation. It discusses in detail the vital ingredients that are universally applicable for explorers of the inner path and it discusses the barriers, detours, and pitfalls that we encounter along the way. This is a companion book to an earlier work, *Silence, Simplicity, and Solitude* (Bell Tower, 1992), which describes how to design a spiritual retreat to gain an environment conducive to inner work.

The advice offered in *The Heart of Stillness* is particularly useful for those who aspire to attain new levels of inner silence that enhance the process of self-discovery. This book draws upon wisdom teachings from a cross-section of traditions, including Buddhism, Christianity, Hinduism, Islam, and Judaism. It combines contemporary knowledge with transmissions from thousands of years ago, which remain as relevant as if the sages were speaking to us face-to-face. I have often felt, as this book took shape, that my own enlightenment process will develop to the extent that I am able to integrate into my life the wisdom offered in these pages. Rather than my being a "teacher" who has written a book, the book has become my teacher.

I would like to acknowledge some of the guides whose presence has been an inspiration for me: Reb. Zalman Schachter, Reb. Shlomo Carlebach; Ram Dass; Pir Vilayat Inayat Khan, Bilal Hyde; Father Theophane, Joseph Goldstein, Jack Kornfield, and Sharon Salzberg.

Many of my spiritual guides are no longer in their physical bodies but remain alive with me through the publication of their offerings. These teachers are too numerous to mention, but I do feel it is important to acknowledge the many authors, editors, and publishers who have provided the general public with the essential teachings of a wide variety of sages. This is often done at considerable personal sacrifice and with little monetary gain because of the belief that it is important to assure the dissemination of these wisdom teachings. As a result, the average person today has at her or his fingertips more resources for spiritual development than ancient kings, emperors, or even erudite scholars of the last century.

Thank you to Toinette Lippe, my editor, who has had the faith and persistence to bring my books to fruition. Also, I wish to express gratitude to my business associate, Alan Secrest, and my wife, Shoshana, who provided support and resources that allowed me to give full attention to the completion of this and my previous book.

# MASTERING
# MONKEY MIND

# MASTERING
# MONKEY MIND

*At the sound of the evening bell, newly arrived retreatants begin to file into the large meditation hall. There are many familiar faces in the crowd, meditators I have seen on numerous retreats over the years. A large number of the retreatants are themselves well-known teachers of meditation.*

*Compared to many of the people in this room, I am still a beginner. Although I have a dozen years of meditation experience and have accumulated thousands of hours on retreat, some of the people here have been retreating many times each year for over thirty or forty years. Yet I have never met anyone who was arrogant about his or her meditative skills. Spiritual retreat is a humbling practice. Indeed, teachers who have been around the longest say that we are all beginners.*

*One of the main Burmese teachers in the Vipassanā\* (a Buddhist school) lineage is here in the West to guide a two-month silent retreat. This retreat was fully booked with over one hundred participants before it was even announced in the newsletter.*

*The organizers of this retreat have laughingly referred to it as "the summit." There have probably never before been so many meditation teachers from around the world gathered together in one place for such*

---

\* In order to help readers pronounce unfamiliar words in other languages, I have added macrons to show which vowels are long. These are the only diacritical marks I have used. Often words are mispronounced because we are unaware of the length of the vowels and which syllables need stressing.

*a long period of time. Other people, like me, heard about this through the grapevine, and registered more than six months ago. We will spend more than a thousand hours together in total silence, never even looking at each other. The prospect of working with this meditation master in a highly disciplined practice drew people like bees to honey.*

These were notes I made while awaiting the welcoming talk on the opening night of an exceptional sixty-day retreat in Barre, Massachusetts. Despite the fact that this was a Buddhist-oriented program, there were people from many religious traditions: a Jesuit monk, a Benedictine who sometimes sat in his robes, a few priests and nuns, a student of Sufism, a teacher in the Hindu lineage, and quite a few Jews. A fair number of the retreatants considered themselves Buddhists, but many others, like myself, frequently use the format of a disciplined retreat to intensify practices that have other roots. Many of us have discovered that deep meditation on extended retreat opens wondrous gates.

Most of the participants came from states around the nation, but many had traveled from abroad. I remember smiling when I heard that a fellow had come from Kathmandu. I could not help but think about all the people who travel to India in the quest for enlightenment, while the man from Kathmandu came to a small town in Massachusetts for a Buddhist retreat. Other nations represented included Germany, Scandinavia, England, Australia, Vietnam, Burma, Thailand, Argentina, and South Africa. My wife and I had come from Jerusalem.

Our daily schedule was simple but austere. We alternated sitting and walking meditation each hour. The first official meditation of each day began at 5:30 A.M., but many people started much earlier. The last sit of the day finished at 10:00 P.M., but, again, many remained in the large, darkened meditation hall until past midnight. I usually began my retreat days between 3:00 and 4:00 A.M.

Eating was also a silent meditation. We maintained mindfulness while lifting and lowering our spoons, chewing, or swallowing. The only time we spoke was when we reported to one of the teachers about our meditation experience. The teachers did not want to know so much about our inner visions, flashing lights, or conversations with angelic beings—those are ordinary fantasies. They were much more interested in how we were dealing with pain or how well we noticed the minute details of the rising and falling of our chests as our breath entered and left our bodies.

My wife, Shoshana, sat on the other side of the large hall. We were prepared not to speak, or even make eye contact, for two months. We had separate sleeping accommodations. The year before this, we had completed forty days of silence in the same retreat center. We have always had good communication, but that forty-day period added a remarkable new depth to our relationship—so much can be said in silence.

During our previous retreat, and at this one as well, Shoshana and I "cheated" a little on Friday evenings. In the Jewish tradition, just before sundown on Friday is the time of lighting the Sabbath candles. Thus, once each week, we met silently in the corner of the dining room to do our little ritual. After lighting, we passed our hands over the flames, gathered the light into our hearts, covered our eyes, and said a silent prayer, just as we do every Sabbath. When we finished, during the first moments after we uncovered our eyes, we sometimes caught a glance, a slight smile, a moment of bonding. This was our only communication for the entire week.

Near the end of these retreats Shoshana quietly returned to my room a few Friday evenings after candle lighting to join me for the traditional blessings over wine and bread. We used grape juice in place of wine because of retreat rules against drugs and intoxicants. We ate in silence, and although we ached to caress each other, we held fast to the house rule of the retreat center—no sex.

A few other couples were also on this retreat, but many of the retreatants had spouses at home watching the kids. I think someone came who did half of the retreat and then changed places so the spouse could attend the other half. People with families find ways to attend such retreats.

At the end of the two months, there was a three-day program designed for younger people, and many of the retreatants' children came at that time. We usually think of retreat as a lone endeavor, but it can also be a family experience.

*Retreatants have filled the room. They entered quietly in bare feet or in stockings, carrying cushions as though they were comfortable, old friends. The hall was set up with mats aligned eight abreast in fourteen rows. After seating themselves, many people threw a shawl or blanket over their shoulders. This act accentuated the feeling for me that each person spun a cocoon of personal solitude in the midst of the crowd. They could dwell in this solitude until the end of the retreat.*

There were about an equal number of men and women. This was an interesting and diverse group, many of whom had to make a considerable effort to set aside two months from their professional careers. Shoshana arrived a couple of days before the retreat began. I had a few weeks head start because I wanted to do an individual twenty-day retreat before the major event. I was fortunate to have extra time for integration so that I could maximize the two-month intensive. This had become my world already, complete in its simplicity.

Not long ago, a meditation teacher told the story of his return from an extended retreat in Southeast Asia. Entering the United States, an official at passport control asked him what he had been doing, and he replied that he was just returning from a long retreat. The official said, "Welcome back to the real world."

What is the real world? When we sit quietly, we discover that everything we thought was real is actually insubstantial. Under close scrutiny, everyday reality collapses into itself. What remains is something quite different from our initial concepts. Moreover, when we sit on an intensive retreat, the external reality often becomes a vague and dim parody of life compared with the vibrancy of our expanded inner vision. Which one is real?

People go on retreat to uncover a new perception, a way of seeing things as they are, rather than as they seem to be. In this environment, people often link together in an unspoken bond, never looking at or speaking to one another, yet concentrated in a unified endeavor to gain insight into the workings of their individual minds. They are there to master what is known in the meditation world as "monkey mind."

*The retreatants have all arrived and are seated on their mats waiting for the appearance of the teacher. There have been a few silent acknowledgments, but the room is still. The rustling noises of people settling on their cushions has stopped and now not even a whisper breaks the silence. Almost everyone has begun to meditate.*

*If this had been an average gathering of retreatants there might have been the fidgeting that accompanies our sense of waiting for something to happen. Most of us believe that a retreat begins when the master enters, or a meditation starts when the bell rings. Some of these more experienced retreatants, however, seem to be meditating even as they walk into the hall, long before they sit down. For them, this is simply an ongoing practice that began long ago. These more experienced meditators and teachers are influencing the rest of us without speaking a word. This is going to be a splendid retreat.*

*I have the feeling that even if the teacher did not show up tonight and the bell never rang, it would not matter much to most people present. They would sit and walk in meditation until the time to sleep, and tomorrow they would return for another session. These people are already deeply committed to dwelling in the heart of stillness.*

The heart of stillness is a concept I learned to appreciate many years ago. When we begin to meditate, we quickly realize how much the mind is chattering. An incessant internal monologue—which often is perceived as a dialogue—is filled with desire, aversion, judgment, criticism, doubt, anxiety, fantasy, illusion, anger, fear, and on and on it goes.

Our busy minds are so much a part of daily life, most of us have come to believe that this is our natural condition. Our thoughts engage the moment. We calculate, analyze, speculate, plan, and reflect; we move with ease and rapidity from subject to subject. Indeed, the mind is a marvelous gift, ingenious, creative, and enormously powerful.

We usually assume we are in control of our minds, but sometimes—more often than we admit to ourselves—we are gripped with obsessions and are oblivious to everything going on around us as thoughts continually repeat themselves. Our emotions may be aroused and we may find ourselves hating someone or furious about an event. As this obsession gains momentum, our thoughts may turn to revenge, and at times we fantasize about harming someone. We may even envision scenes filled with violence that repeat over and over again. Who is in control during those runaway fantasies?

Even though an angry mind state may capture us completely, most of us have an unconscious "suppressor" that prevents us from causing physical injury to others during our mental rage. However, we have no way to measure how much harm we do to ourselves. Mental violence, whether acted out or not, still releases bile and other gastric juices, and extra adrenaline pumps through the body. The effect of our thoughts on our health remains a major unexplored territory in medicine.

While anger is obvious, other subtle mind states also influence us and our bodies react as though the event or situation we imagine is actually happening. We breathe more heavily and erratically when we are anxious. Our blood flow changes when we have fearful thoughts, and our hands may tremble nervously. We can feel a grip in our abdomen when we reflect on a criticism. Each mental reflection is like adhesive flypaper that binds us in its own universe until another thought pulls us away; each universe leaves a residue of glue that sticks in our minds even after we manage to pull free. We cannot shake off this gummy mess of jumbled thoughts.

Only in moments of silence and solitude do we discover that the mind is more often than not running on its own track. Not only one track, but many that crisscross. Sometimes we are familiar with the region our minds visit; at others we seem to harbor the thoughts of strangers. The closer we pay attention to the mind, the more outrageous it becomes, and eventually we realize that we are hardly ever in control. In that awareness we must face the truth that we are more confused than we think—we are more like homo simians than homo sapiens, we live most of our lives in the jungle of monkey mind.

This idea of "monkey mind" is a well-known concept in Eastern traditions. It is not familiar to most of us in the West, but it is an important idea that needs to be expressed. We have all experienced active, nervous minds, when our thoughts seem to jump rapidly as though from one branch to another. Often the thoughts are contradictory or confused; we vacillate to extremes. Our mental process is frequently just like monkeys we see in a zoo; dashing here and there, jumping, grabbing, swinging, and screeching.

Humankind suffers the normal consequences of its ignorance, but our unbridled minds greatly accentuate the errors we make. Most of us do not realize the degree to which monkey mind dominates our thoughts throughout the day, constantly unsettling the foundation of our conceptual framework. If we cannot gain an understanding of our individual process, how can we hope for the collective thought of humanity to be any different?

Every aspect of the quality of life is affected by our frame of mind: relationships, health, the way we raise children, satisfaction with work, and our sense of purpose. In our worst nightmares, we consider what life would be like under a dictator who obliterates personal freedom. But we miss the greatest tyrant in everyday life: monkey mind! Free-flowing thoughts can be our greatest asset when we are in a creative mode, but when an unruly mental process limits our awareness, the mind becomes an oppressor.

If we interrupt ourselves at any time during the day and

ask, "What is happening in my mind at this very moment?" we will almost always encounter monkey mind. If we are worried about something, thinking over a recent conversation, hoping an event will go a certain way, troubled about our appearance, wishing a person would act differently, or any of a thousand familiar ruminations, we are in a jungle without much light. We have tricked ourselves into believing we need to think about these things. We have conditioned ourselves to be comfortable when engaged in thought, we are uncomfortable when we try to ignore thoughts as they arise. Indeed, the mind functions by grasping at floating thoughts, holding on to them, working with them, and discarding them only when a replacement thought arises.

"What is wrong with this?" we may wonder. "If this is the way the mind functions, what is the problem?" The answer is that although we have learned to control most of our natural functions, we have done little to control the mind. When we see something sweet to eat, our inclination is to reach out, grasp it, and put it in our mouths. Yet, we know if we eat too many sweets, we become ill. We are aware of limitations like this. We have learned that almost any excess is unhealthy, but when it comes to the mind, anything goes.

It is easy to experience monkey mind in action. Stop reading for five minutes and pay close attention to the thoughts that arise. We sometimes notice our thoughts more readily when we try to concentrate on one thing. Think of a word or look at an object, and try to concentrate on this word or object for five minutes. This is not as easy as it sounds; soon the mind begins to wander. Welcome to monkey mind. No matter how much we try to narrow our focus, the mind switches back and forth between channels, constantly branching into associations as it weaves through a complex matrix of thought processes.

Some writers, like James Joyce, have recorded this mode of thought in a technique that is known as "stream of consciousness." In a way, this is a misnomer because we are not really conscious of our thoughts when they are being tossed about like this. True consciousness is related to awareness, while this river of scattered thought actually blankets our awareness. Try it out. Take five minutes and watch your thoughts. You will discover that you quickly become lost in random thought, forget that you are trying to observe your mental process, and are caught time and again by monkey mind.

Fortunately, there is a remedy. Monkey mind holds power over us only to the extent that we believe it is the normal flow of our life process. It is not. Many spiritual teachers have transmitted to us that we live far below our potential, miss most of what is going on around us, and exist in a world of illusion. They teach that peace of mind is our natural heritage and that we can awaken this potential within us at any time.

Entering the heart of stillness and discovering inner peace is a central focus for people who do spiritual work. Many years ago, when I first heard of people sitting in silence for days or weeks at a time, I wondered why intelligent people would put themselves through so much self-deprivation and discomfort. I now know the secret shared by most serious meditators and retreatants— something known and practiced for thousands of years. The secret is this: monkey mind feeds in darkness, it shrinks under the light of observation.

This may not sound so momentous at first. Most people have the chatter of monkey mind as a constant companion, have no direct experience of anything else, and thus have little incentive to see what happens to the mind when the noise within stops. However, those who taste the sweetness of this inner silence realize a more profound awareness than anything previously experienced. Indeed, the beam of self-observation that destroys monkey mind has its source in what is commonly called "enlightenment."

Enlightenment continues to be the most misunderstood concept of the spiritual quest. It has been known by many names: *nirvāna, satori, kenshō,* cosmic consciousness, transcendental awareness, or even heaven. Enlightenment is often used these days in a simplistic context that drains it of meaning. Our misconception of it and our striving toward an ephemeral idea we cannot grasp is a formidable barrier along the spiritual path.

There has been so much written about enlightenment, we could defend almost any idea of what the term means. If we equate enlightenment with *nirvāna,* we see it defined in the Hindu tradition as the "final absorption in Brahman, or the All-pervading reality, by the annihilation of the individual ego"; and in the Buddhist tradition as "the ultimate stage of realization according to the teachings of the Buddha."[1]

In Zen, we can have experiences of enlightenment called *satori* or *kenshō.* These words are interchangeable and are defined as "opening the Mind's eye, awakening to one's True-nature and hence to the nature of all existence."[2] Philip Kapleau, author of *The Three Pillars of Zen,* suggests that the term *satori* implies a deeper realization and is customarily used only when describing the Buddha and the patriarchs, while *kenshō* is the language we use when talking about our own experiences.[3]

Although hardly anyone suggests they have attained the exalted state of *nirvāna* described above, many Zen practitioners have had the experience of *kenshō,* either in a momentary flash or as a frequent occurrence. Kapleau's teacher, Yasutani, said, "When you have *kenshō* you see into the world of oneness, or equality, and this realization can be either shallow or deep; usually a first *kenshō* is shallow."[4] This idea of a "shallow" enlightenment is another fork in the winding road we enter when trying to define the term.

Some teachers talk about *samādhi,* but this too has a wide spectrum of definitions. One teacher describes the idea of a "blissful superconscious state in which a yogi perceives the identity of the individualized soul and Cosmic Spirit."[5] But there is also the idea of a lower and higher form of *samādhi.* The lower form is called *sabikalpa samādhi,* where "the devotee's consciousness merges in the Cosmic Spirit . . . the body . . . [is] motionless and rigid. The yogi is fully aware of his bodily condition of suspended animation."[6] The higher form is called *nirbikalpa samādhi,* where "he communes with God without bodily fixation . . . even in the midst of exacting worldly duties."[7]

The growth of Buddhism in the West over the last thirty years has put a different cast on the idea of *samādhi.* Here the emphasis is much more on concentration than cosmic consciousness. One book says, "*Samādhi* is the state of concentrated calm resulting from meditation practice."[8] In another, we find "It implies not merely equilibrium, tranquillity, and one-pointedness, but a state of intense yet effortless concentration, of complete absorption of the mind itself, of heightened and expanded awareness."[9]

Although these are but a few of hundreds of definitions, we are already confused. Enlightenment fits the category of unusual subjects about which the more we read and the more we study, the less we understand.

> *A fifty-year-old student of enlightenment said to Shinkan [a thirteenth-century Buddhist teacher], "I have studied the Tendai [a Buddhist sect that originated in China] school of thought since I was a little boy, but one thing in it I cannot understand. Tendai claims that even the trees and grass will become enlightened. To me this seems very strange."*
>
> *"Of what use is it to discuss how grass and trees become enlightened?" asked Shinkan. "The question is how you yourself can become so. Did you ever consider that?"*
>
> *"I never thought of it that way," marveled the old man.*
>
> *"Then go home and think it over," finished Shinkan.*[10]

This simple story teaches us we cannot learn about enlightenment except through our own experience. This is why we use the word *practice* when discussing spiritual endeavor—it means being engaged, acquiring direct experience. Such experiences are not intellectual and thus they are almost impossible to share using concepts. Most questions about enlightenment are unanswerable. Understanding arises out of silence rather than words.

Another major obstacle for beginning meditators is fascination with magic or occult powers. Enlightenment is sometimes mistakenly viewed as a capacity we can acquire, a mechanism that provides miraculous strength to its possessor, a panacea for all ills, or a magical potion that will ward off all trouble. Most people recognize the folly in this, but there are those who hope that the benefits of spiritual work include clairvoyance or psychic ability. We do indeed encounter new parts of ourselves by stripping away the veils of our slumber; we become aware of our essential character and are opened to capabilities beyond limits self-imposed through ignorance, but these abilities must never be the goal of our work. Here is an excellent Buddhist story on this issue:

> One day the Buddha came across an ascetic who sat by the bank of a river, and who had practiced austerities for twenty-five years. The Buddha asked him what he had got out of all his labor. The ascetic proudly replied that now at last he could cross the river by walking on the water. The Buddha tried to point out that this was little gain for so much labor, since for one penny the ferry would take him across.[11]

The quest for magical powers almost always leads to a cul-de-sac; we may think we have attained something, but really we have become caught in another delusion. Enlightenment is not something magical but is related to the idea that we have a deeply rooted desire to uncover the secret of our own existence, understand our purpose, and continue on the path of perfecting ourselves. This impetus of all spiritual endeavor has dramatically influenced the process of human development. Masters know "enlightenment" is a verb rather than a noun. It is not a state, but a process. Enlightenment does not end with an attainment; it is a continuous unfolding.

Many teachers have said that the enlightened mind is our primal nature. Our active, busy minds continually push away this enlightened state. When we find a way to quiet the mind, then awareness immediately expands and fills the vacuum. Thus the simple idea expressed earlier, that monkey mind shrinks under the light of observation, is really the secret of the enlightenment process itself. Mastering monkey mind is nothing less than the most direct enlightenment path available to every spiritual aspirant.

A retreat has often been equated with climbing a mountain. Committed mountain climbers have no choice but to face the challenge of the next climb. As they gain more expertise, they learn to use their equipment to attempt increasingly difficult objectives. An outside observer sees only the strenuous effort and the raw conditions of wind, rain, sleet, and freezing temperatures. Those of us who are not climbers cannot help but wonder, "Why do they do it?" The mountaineers occasionally may also ask the same question, but only fleetingly. They have a deeper knowing, a satisfaction, a feeling that transcends all inquiry.

Participants in an arduous retreat experience a similar depth of commitment. Retreats can be difficult. There may be the physical pain involved in sitting quietly, or the psychological pain of facing ourselves as masks drop away. In addition, a retreatant must cope with boredom, loneliness, and all the attendant fears of being out of social contact.

What follows is taken from notes I wrote near the end of the summit retreat:

*The retreat rhythms here have become a way of life. A few weeks ago, I felt awed by the majesty of nature. I could hardly take a step without being overwhelmed by an explosion of sensations. Now I am undergoing a different experience—there is no separation between "me" and "not-me," between subject and object. Therefore no "me" exists to be overwhelmed by something outside of myself. This body walking is the same as the butterfly fluttering, the beetle ambling, the snake slithering, the wind moving. This body breathing feels like sunrise and sunset, bird wings flapping, sounds rising and falling.*

*We give names to these experiences in order to communicate. But the experiences are not these names, nor do ideas contain them. They are experiences that come and go. But the feeling within is a constant "at oneness," nothing separate, nothing to ponder, everything in its place, as it should be, just right, perfect.*

*To say that this is the most complete peace is an understatement.*

*This is far beyond peace, harmony, balance, love—it is unspeakable.*
*This experience transcends anything I could have imagined and is so*
*overwhelming nothing could replace it. Not all the power, money, sex,*
*or fame—nothing, including the threat of death, is bigger than this.*

*But I am not giving an accurate picture if I dwell on these sublime*
*feelings. Just yesterday, I had many strenuous meditations. I spun out*
*of control and at one point I wanted to get up and walk out of the room.*
*It was painful. Fantasies poured over each other in a cascade of images;*
*everything seemed to be going wrong. I felt that all of my time had been*
*wasted. At this moment life is glorious, but I know that later today,*
*tomorrow, or the day after I could drop into another morass.*

*Peace beyond comprehension following hell realms of my own*
*making. It was unpleasant yesterday, but now that seems so distant, so*
*irrelevant.*

*I feel energy gathering for the next sit. I hear an almost*
*imperceptible footstep in the hallway. Subtle lights and shadows*
*playing against my window reflect human movement on the lawn.*
*Soon the distant sound of the bell will announce another period of*
*sitting. I have given up counting the days. It matters not. I am so*
*thankful for the peace, the peace, the sublime peace.*

"Is it worth it?"—the question so often asked—has no
answer. The response would depend upon when it was
being asked. In a moment of discomfort, we may have
serious doubts. In a moment of ecstatic release, the
question is absurd. Once we have experienced this release,
we are never quite the same. We may briefly think about
quitting, but we cannot. A seed that sprouts can never be
a seed again; it must have nourishment to grow or it will
die. This is a universal law, and it applies to the spiritual
quest. We all hold these seeds. Once aroused, we have no
alternative but to continue the process.

An observer walking up and down the aisles of meditators during the "summit" retreat would not have

learned much. He or she would have seen only a group of people sitting quietly. On the lawns outside the meditation hall, the observer would have noticed some people walking slowly, carefully, while others were pacing back and forth like tigers in a cage. There would be nothing to learn from all of this because the real adventure was taking place inside the minds of these experienced meditators and teachers.

During that retreat, it occurred to me that if all the resources of the meditators and teachers in that hall could be accumulated, the result would benefit spiritual explorers for a long time to come. I resolved to gather together a variety of teachings others might use while on retreat— material I wished I had had when I began on my spiritual path.

We know we cannot fully perceive what goes on in another's mind, yet wisdom teachings extend back for thousands of years on how to work with different mind states as they arise. This is really what we want to know because it would help us understand how to work with our own thoughts and emotions.

Many people have written about their spiritual insights and retreat experiences. Most of these writings are limited by the parameters of the writer's traditional path: Buddhist practices, Hindu practices, Christian, Jewish, or Sufi practices. But my experience has been that universal principles of spiritual practice apply to all of us.

Thus, by exploring the principles of inner work, we are able to gain insight into how experienced retreatants deal with thoughts and mind states that usually disturb less practiced meditators. These principles apply not only to meditation but to all life experience. Once we learn how to cope with fear, pain, anger, or other thoughts that appear in a retreat setting, we can use the same methods in everyday life. Moreover, the elements of spiritual practice—purification, concentration, effort, and mastery —are the same qualities we need to integrate into our lives for more balanced and harmonious living.

Sometimes when we learn a new word, we begin to see that word frequently for the next few weeks. The word was always there, of course, but once we are paying more attention, it is highlighted in our awareness. The same is true of teachings about how the mind works. Once we gain insight into the makeup of our thoughts and emotions, how they work, and what we can do to relieve ourselves, distracting mind states have less potency to capture and imprison us. Therefore, as we read this book, we need not wait for a time of spiritual practice; the teachings can be applied to all our daily activities.

We quickly discover, however, that a constant discipline is difficult to sustain. Although we are able to observe our uncontrolled thought processes whenever we wish, it will take a long-term commitment to defeat our monkey minds. In the same way, we can learn important lessons about dealing with fear, anger, boredom, or many other mind states, but we will still be trapped by them over and over again. In many other endeavors, once we understand how a process works, we learn not to repeat the same mistake. On the spiritual path, however, our habitual and conditioned behavior is so deeply ingrained that we continue to confront teachings we have already experienced, and we slip into old tendencies that have already borne bitter fruit. We are slow to learn.

This is why we usually adopt spiritual practices. We must "recondition" ourselves. Just knowing the truth is not sufficient. The wisdom of the sages is always deceptively simple. "Be here now," "Love thy neighbor," "Trust in God," "Do not do unto others that which you would not have them do unto you"—we all know these wisdom teachings, and dozens of others. Do we live our lives directed by any of them?

Spiritual practice is the attempt to integrate into our lives wisdom that has been transmitted through the ages. A retreat is an intensification of spiritual practice. Thus, we will direct our attention in this book to the process of spiritual retreat as a paradigm from which we can learn how to do all spiritual practice. The goal is not that we should necessarily learn to be good retreatants, but that we incorporate the wisdom teachings so we can more fully live our everyday lives free of monkey mind.

The next section of the book describes the elements of spiritual practice. These are the foundation stones of our spiritual work. The third section of the book addresses the negative mind states we encounter in our life experience, which become more immediate when we undertake intense practices such as retreats. The tools we utilize to subdue these negative mind states are useful both on retreat and in our daily lives. Finally, the last section of the book discusses positive mind states, which at first glance seem to be the goal of spiritual practice, but often are roadblocks to our continuing development. Thus, this book is useful for each reader, whether just beginning on the path or deeply involved in the exploration of the inner universe.

NOTE: The "summit" retreat took place in the spring of 1988 at the Insight Meditation Society, Barre, Massachusetts, under the direction of the Venerable U Pandita Sayadaw and his staff from Rangoon, Burma. Those who have never experienced a retreat and would like to know more about the method of arranging one will find specific guidance in my book, *Silence, Simplicity, and Solitude* (Bell Tower, 1992).

# THE
# FOUNDATION OF
# SPIRITUAL
# PRACTICE

# INTRODUCTION

Spiritual practices are as diverse as the number of cultures recorded in the archives of human endeavor. Such practices are based on mythology, ideology, or cosmology, and are influenced by cultural mores, psychology, social patterning, climate, seasons, agriculture, and even geographical location. Some people pray aloud, chant repetitive phrases, or eschew all forms of prayer; some sit quietly resting the eyes and mind on a single object. Others dance, paint their bodies, pierce their skin, use totems, eat special foods, light fires, make physical gestures, sprinkle water, study scriptures, sacrifice animals, or discuss imponderables. The list grows with every new anthropological study.

We have a tendency to form judgments about other people's practices. Some practices may be viewed as primitive or archaic, others as idolatrous or perverted, childish or bizarre, immoral or foolish. Yet, if we have any spiritual inclination ourselves, and are willing to be honest, we will find traces of these same practices in our own belief system or in the way our individual religious traditions are expressed.

It should neither surprise nor dismay us to find an overlap between primitive religious expression and modern spiritual practice—the power hidden in our primal resources is our key to gateways otherwise closed. Most of our modern traditions have roots in primitive practice. Even if we are not adherents of religious beliefs that go back hundreds or thousands of years, but follow a brand-new twentieth-century avenue of spiritual inquiry, the practices we invent will still have a commonality with spiritual endeavor undertaken in many parts of the world, whether in aboriginal cultures or sophisticated communities. Moreover, we will find elements of these practices recorded throughout history.

Only a limited number of foundation principles have been uncovered, despite the large number of studies carried out among diverse cultures around the world. In other words, our efforts to gain an understanding of life's purpose, or to perfect ourselves and the world around us, have common denominators with spiritual practices of many different peoples.

There are at least four essential elements composing the foundation of the enlightenment process: purification, concentration, effort, and mastery. It is helpful for us to evaluate our practice by the criteria of one or more of these essential characteristics.

In addition, when we understand the purpose of these elements, we gain a fresh appreciation of many different practices and traditions because we are better prepared to see the universality in the process of spiritual inquiry. This deepens our own inner work and helps us to respect others.

# PURIFICATION

An underlying principle of all spiritual practice is purification. The process of purification is based on the idea that our essential nature is already pure, and enlightenment is the inborn condition of life. The only reason we do not experience our inherent enlightened state is because our essential being remains hidden behind veils that keep us in a dreamlike condition. Once these veils are removed, we awaken to the ever-present illumination. The metaphor of sleep and awakening, or veils filtering out the light, is common in the language of spiritual endeavor. Another often-used metaphor concerns the idea of the "stuff" we all haul around, which is often referred to as "baggage."

Every meditator carries an enormous amount of baggage in the form of mental static. This provides fuel for noisy thought-engines that seem to be constantly running. We enter life with relatively little of this baggage, perhaps only enough to fill a small briefcase. Along the way, we pick up large sacks of emotions, steamer trunks of disappointment, and moving vans of experiences. To all this we cling.

In adult life, it often feels as though the baggage is passing through our daily consciousness on a long freight train, with no caboose in sight. This is a clear image for many of us. We are standing on a path waiting to cross the tracks. The gate is down, the red lights are flashing, the bells are ringing. Passing in front of us is the longest train anyone has ever seen. It is filled with memories, reflections, planning, constant chatter, and repeating patterns. There we stand, waiting to cross. We are not able to turn back or go around. Unless the gate opens, we may stand and wait forever.

If we look down the track from the direction the train is approaching, we will see that the reason the freight train seems so long is because somebody is constantly slipping in new boxcars. Indeed, if we explore our baggage of jumbled thoughts, we will discover that much of it has been added recently. Plenty of old, creaking boxcars continue serving this freight train, but the bulk of the train is composed of newly added stock. And, behold, the "somebody" who is adding new boxcars of baggage looks just like us.

It does not take long to figure out that we will never see the caboose as long as the train is being replenished. We are constantly taking on fresh baggage at many levels. Our desires alone account for an enormous load, not to speak of our judging minds or our grasping for a personal identity. These attitudes will be discussed later—the concern here is the kind of baggage that sticks to us as the result of our unconscious behavior. All our actions, speech, and thoughts have the potential for accumulating short- or long-term baggage that may interfere with our spiritual work.

The most elementary aspect of purification pertains to minimizing and ultimately eliminating actions, speech, and thought processes that leave residual baggage. This first level of spiritual work is to get to the source, to stop creating more burdens when we already have enough to keep us busy for a long time to come.

Morality and virtue are usually associated with religious beliefs, providing ideals for humankind. We learn in our early training that we should perform certain acts because they are "right," and avoid others because they are "wrong." It seems arbitrary to us when we are children, but we get the message that rightness has rewards while wrongness is punished.

In the last few hundred years, the so-called Age of Enlightenment, we have witnessed a potent challenge to the ideas of right and wrong. It is as though the child in us was correct in the first place, and under scrutiny the arbitrary edifice of morality and virtue crumbles. Anthropological studies prove that morality is relative—what is good for me may not be good for you. As a result, there has been a great deal of confusion in the last century as to which principles, if any, are imperative for humanity, and which should be eradicated because they are based on ignorance or are intrinsically harmful.

This is perhaps one of our most challenging questions. Is there a need for a moral authority? Are there principles that can be generally applied for the betterment of humankind, or should we accept everything as relative and constantly adjust our moral perspective to the needs of the times? As with all difficult questions, there is a tendency for individuals on both sides to carry their beliefs to an extreme. Those who are strict adherents of moral authority tend to build a clearly defined structure that can be used to measure everything in terms of virtue, while those who believe everything is relative tend to find a potential for good or evil in every action.

Obviously, this is an enormous subject, which is beyond the scope of this book. However, it is crucial to note that mystics in every tradition presume virtue and morality to be the bedrock upon which all spiritual aspiration is based. They are not concerned with a philosophical or sociological analysis of right and wrong, nor is it a question of morality imposed by religious authority. Mystics see virtue and morality as an absolute necessity in practice, and this is rapidly verified through direct experience. Without following virtuous principles, the mind becomes hopelessly clouded, and the spiritual aspirant remains stuck in a murky abyss, thrashing about in the darkness.

The esoteric approach to virtuous behavior concentrates on the way our thoughts are affected by the actions we perform or the words we utter. Obviously, a conscious or unconscious process precedes our actions and speech. Even a reflex is a reaction to a stimulus. Somewhat less obvious, however, is the fact that each action itself has implications that affect our thought process.

For example, we must have some consciousness and motivation to reach across the dinner table for the salt. When our sleeve brushes a milk glass and knocks it over, we have an instant opportunity to observe how our actions affect our thoughts. The same holds true for more subtle implications: the internal buildup for every word or action is like mist evaporating from our mental pond, but our actual speech or action may be represented as raindrops splashing back into the pond, causing reverberations. After a downpour, our mind pond may settle quickly or it may be disrupted for quite some time—indeed, a chain reaction may be initiated that amplifies our mental activity for hours or days.

This relationship between action and thought is at the core of the mystic's emphasis on virtuous behavior. As we become more exacting in the minutiae of life, the greater our spiritual refinement and awareness. And as we become more aware, we appreciate the necessity of being meticulous in our actions.

In Buddhism, the principle of virtue is a prerequisite for all enlightenment endeavor. The well-known Eightfold Path can be condensed into three basic areas: *sīla* (virtue); *samādhi* (concentration); and *panna* (wisdom). The aspect of virtue underlies all potential for achieving high states of wisdom.

A contemporary Buddhist monk, Bhikkhu Suruttama, writes,

> *Whatever one's path, the practice of* dhamma [*Pali: generally meaning "the way," or "the law"; in Sanskrit:* dharma] *is built upon a foundation of* sīla—*virtue, integrity, and purity of both behavior and speech. Without the foundation of* sīla, *one's life and mind become filled with agitation and regrets—obstructions to clarity, tranquillity, and insight. Thus,* sīla *creates the space in which the entire Path of practice can unfold.*
>
> Sīla *should not be confused with externally imposed commandments. Rather, it is the voluntary undertaking of commitments that harmonize our actions and speech with the principles by which the universe operates, thereby bringing harmony, peace, and happiness to our lives and minds.*"[1]

Virtue and morality that is legislated, either through religious obligation or by the law of the land, maintains social order and religious cohesion, but it may also become dogma or a tool for intimidation. It is not particularly useful for the spiritual aspirant.

The idea of "voluntary" acceptance of commitment, however, is not appropriate. To the extent we are free agents and can choose to participate in a religion, tradition, or spiritual path, we make a voluntary choice. Each choice, however, carries with it a degree of responsibility to abide by the accepted principles of the designated path.

THE FOUNDATION OF SPIRITUAL PRACTICE

Every path has its own rules, its own "commandments." We can choose whether or not to play by the rules of the game, but if we choose not to, we need to seek out another game.

At the beginning of a Theravāda Buddhist retreat, participants are invited to accept five basic precepts for the period of the retreat: not to kill, steal, engage in sex, lie, or take intoxicants. This appears relatively straight-forward at first. That is, until we find out that not to kill means not to swat a mosquito, not to step on an ant, not to put out poison for rodent control, or spray to keep the cockroach population down. It does not take long before some of our sensibilities are confronted.

More advanced retreatants in the Theravāda form may not eat any solid food after noon (until the next morning), use makeup or perfume, or sleep on a bed more than a few inches above the ground. The number of precepts increases as a person becomes more committed to the process. For monks, 227 precepts must be observed.

Precepts work on the basic level of morality and virtue; they are directed toward minimizing the addition of new mental burdens that result from unskillful actions or speech. This is an essential element of the purification process, which, as we shall see, is made up of three rudimentary principles: avoidance of harmful acts, surrender, and personal sacrifice.

The starting point for all purification processes is to avoid actions that literally harm other life forms. Destructive acts such as killing or stealing have immediate implications. The most obvious results occur when the act is a crime and society demands justice. The more subtle implications arise from those actions which do not fit the criminal code of society, yet are an offense against nature or universal law.

Many examples exist of legal harmful actions. Every aspect of relationship, work, parenting, and life in general offers continuous opportunities for subtle, harmful action. A great deal of attention is currently focused on action that is harmful to the environment. Activists point out the effects of such actions on the future of humankind. This is obvious for everyone involved in spiritual work. The mystic goes one step further, however, making the point that not only are people at risk from every destructive act, but the individual who perpetrates the act immediately suffers the effect of constricted awareness.

This concept is not something we can measure, nor can we understand it logically. Our awareness may be awakened by an image of the grief of a swan that has lost its lifetime mate to a hunter more than by an appeal to our reason. Rather than the scientific approach that describes the effects of diminished forests, our awareness may be aroused by meditating on the death throes of a defoliated tree. The unaware person who performs a destructive act suffers subtle experiences like these, and the resultant metaphysical pain causes his or her awareness to diminish even more. This is the mystical perspective.

A Hasidic teaching relates that the gates of heaven are often locked, but tears always find their way in. What are the tears of the lonely swan or the dying tree? What other forms may these tears take? And what is the price heaven will demand for justice? The more sensitive we become in our practice, the more we experience the power that simple destructive acts have to disturb our inner harmony, and the more we become attuned to the true meaning of the interrelationship of everything in the universe.

A common phenomenon in an intensive retreat is the sudden memory of a destructive act long forgotten. At the time we performed it, it may have seemed trivial; it may even have transpired in a way that eluded our consciousness. Yet, when we sit in silence, the experience arises as though it were happening at that very moment. Our sense of remorse can be overwhelming, and the realization that follows can often lead to enormous grief as the hidden pain is released.

Thus, from a meditative perspective, every act has immediate and long-range implications. The avoidance of harmful acts helps to keep the slate clean from this moment on. We can then focus our attention on making amends for past actions. Although the task of cleaning up the past may seem impossible, when we are able to give it our full attention—without the distractions of new burdens—we begin to repair prior damage, thereby merging more deeply into the heart of stillness.

The next principle of purification is surrender. We often encounter rules in spiritual work that do not seem to be rational. What difference does it make whether we sleep on a high bed or a low one? What does it matter if we stop eating at noon, the middle of the afternoon, or when it is dark? Our logical minds seek out relevance, meaning, and purpose. But in the principle of surrender, logic does not apply. Even though an ostensibly nonsensical and artificial rule may turn out to have an important foundation, this is not the justification for the power of surrender. Rather, the point is that surrender and letting go are crucial initial steps in the enlightenment process, for surrender requires a confrontation with our "self"-identification.

A primary goal of spiritual work is to recognize our identification with and attachment to our thoughts. The identification with the thought of "me," or "I am thinking," creates a feeling of separation between the sense of "me" and all that is not "me." When we surrender to a teacher or an ideal, this barrier of separation begins to dissolve. Surrender means letting go of control.

When we first attempt to surrender, there may be great discomfort and insecurity—we have no confidence when we are not in control. After a while, we realize that we were never really in control and that personal control is an illusion. When this understanding comes we gain a new confidence in the flow of the universe, and we are able to harmonize with our surroundings in a fresh way.

Every element of spiritual endeavor requires surrender. The act of yielding helps to prevent new baggage being added because we are no longer acting solely for ourselves. Surrender is also effective on the higher levels of purification, which will be discussed more fully in the chapter on effort.

While surrender is an imperative in the enlightenment process, it also has a troubling potential. Naive spiritual aspirants too often surrender to an individual or ideal that actually leads them astray. The issue of discernment is one of the thorniest questions on the spiritual path. Discernment and surrender can be in opposition to one another, for the identified self often uses discernment to avoid surrender. On the other hand, surrender without some level of discernment is an invitation to disaster.

This interaction between discernment and surrender is part of the continuous fine-tuning that takes place in the enlightenment process. We learn that surrender is not a one-time event but a demand that repeats itself over and over again. We use our discernment as best we can, learning where to hold back and where to yield. There are no absolutes here. This is a spiritual dance that we will be perfecting throughout our lives.

A third principle has to do with sacrifice. The idea of

sacrifice as a form of purification is related to the scientific concept of "conservation of energy." The theory is that despite the degree to which matter is altered from one form to another, the sum total of energy in the universe remains the same. The theory of the conservation of energy has its mystical parallel. The metaphysical principle relates to the "energy" of giving and receiving: We cannot receive without giving and we cannot give without receiving.

In kabbalistic terms, each aspect of creation is a vessel filled to its brim with metaphysical light. This light comes from an infinite Bestower whose essential attribute could be described as having the "will to give." The essential quality of a vessel is the "will to receive." The vessel we call a human being has something very special, it has some of the qualities of the Bestower—it can give that which it receives. But, as soon as a space is created through giving, the emptiness is immediately replenished by the infinite Bestower. However, it is important to realize that an essential difference exists between *wanting* to receive something and *creating* the true potential to receive. A true potential to receive is created only through giving.

The concealed treasures of this principle become profound when we fully appreciate that the art of giving necessitates something to receive our gift, and this act of giving establishes within us an increased potential to receive the light of the infinite Bestower. It is a cycle whereby the source of giving remains at the center, and we are but vehicles through which the light is transmitted. A true understanding of this principle helps to change our relationship with life from our natural receptive mode into one that is more giving—we gain assurance that the wellspring of creative energy is infinite. This contemplation has been a source of inspiration for spiritual explorers for hundreds of years.

When we sacrifice something, we give something up. We may appear to receive less in return because we do not have the awareness to appreciate that our vessel—the part of us which gives—is instantly refilled. It is a principle of purification that when we make a sacrifice, we receive some spiritual reward. The sacrifice does not have to be something material: it could be contributing our time, making a special effort, or letting go of status.

However, the expectation of receiving a reward will transform the nature of the sacrifice. We are not rewarded in the same way if our sacrifice is made with any thought for ourselves. Intention plays a predominant role in esoteric principles. Hence, a purely motivated sacrifice has profound spiritual implications and tremendous purification value.

Most traditional laws and so-called commandments are really aspects of purification that fit into one or more of these three categories: they limit harmful actions, encourage surrender, or require some degree of personal sacrifice.

Someone who rejects a body of traditional law because it makes no sense is missing the point. Esoteric laws are not necessarily understandable by the rational mind. They are designed to help the process of purification, to free us from disturbances, to minimize or eliminate the addition of psychic baggage. Purification moves us closer to liberation.

Ramana Maharshi was once asked, "How does one acquire a strong mind?" He responded, "By the practice of virtue."[2] In the Hindu tradition, this teaching goes back at least two thousand years, to Patanjali, the grandfather of a systematic approach to yoga. Of his eight principles, the first two are: *yama* (conduct regarding others) and *niyama* (conduct regarding oneself).

> Yama *is fulfilled by noninjury to others, truthfulness, nonstealing, continence, and noncovetousness. The* niyama *prescripts are purity of body and mind, contentment in all circumstances, self-discipline, self-study (contemplation), and devotion to God and guru.*[3]

The Sufis have often been suspected by Islamic orthodoxy because of their irreverent approach to the *sharia*, the Islamic body of law. Yet the Sufis are not only observant Muslims, they have additional practices of purification. The most famous set of rules was drawn up by Abu Said ibn Abil-Khayr (tenth century), who was said to have practiced great asceticism for seven years, at times hanging upside-down in a dark well while praying and reciting the Koran.[4]

Abu Said advocated the following principles: 1) maintaining personal cleanliness and a constant state of ritual purity; 2) not gossiping in holy places; 3) praying in congregations; 4) praying often at night; 5) praying for forgiveness at dawn; 6) keeping silence from early morning until sunrise while reading the Koran; 7) practicing a special meditation and mantra in the evening, between the two prayers; 8) welcoming and caring for the poor and needy; 9) not eating alone; and 10) not being absent from the spiritual community without the leader's permission.[5]

Over the centuries there have been many different disciplines, some having common themes, and some not. For example, Pythagoras, who founded a major mystical school in ancient Greece, had a peculiar set of rules, including: 1) abstaining from beans; 2) not picking up what has fallen; 3) not touching a white cock; 4) not breaking bread; 5) not stepping over a crossbar; 6) not stirring the fire with iron; 7) not eating from a whole loaf; 8) not plucking a garland; 9) not sitting on a quart measure; 10) not eating the heart of an animal; 11) not walking on highways; 12) not letting the swallows share one's roof; 13) not leaving the mark of a pot in ashes; 14) not looking in a mirror beside a light; and 15) rolling up bedding immediately upon rising.[6]

Bertrand Russell notes, "All these precepts belong to primitive taboo-conceptions."[7] As the Pythagorean ideal is so distant from us, it may be difficult to cut through the superstition and appreciate its spiritual level. Although most of us cannot relate to the Pythagorean rules, even today cults and esoteric fringe groups have similar taboos.

The more established traditions also have their share of purification practices that are difficult for the uninitiated to comprehend, but the aim is clearly toward higher values. We can get an immediate sense of the thrust of a group's relationship to spirituality by assessing its purification practices. An emphasis on equanimity will reflect one kind of practice, while focus on coming close to God another. Before embracing a spiritual practice we should ask ourselves: Are the practices imbued with magic, superstition, and taboo, or do they show qualities that have immediate benefit for the practitioner and humanity as a whole, like the basic Buddhist, Christian, Hindu, Islamic, or Jewish precepts?

In Judaism, for example, great emphasis is placed on high ideals. In Jerusalem during the eighteenth century, there was a kabbalistic group known as Bet El, the house of God. The group observed a set of practices which included helping each other in every way; working to elevate each other's souls in this world and the world to come; praising one another but never raising anyone higher than any other, even if he was older or wiser; never completely rising as a sign that one was superior to the other when an associate came into a room but rising partway out of respect; never being annoyed with each other; always forgiving with the whole heart and soul; never revealing these precepts to anyone outside the group.[8]

An offshoot of this kabbalistic group still continues to function in Jerusalem. Notice that every element of these practices is involved with relationship, typical of mainstream Judaism which frowns on separation from the community. For traditional Jews, every aspect of life presents itself as a purification practice. An abundance of Jewish laws are directed to raising the holy sparks of purity out of the impure shells that contain them.

A traditional Jew begins with 613 precepts, the foundation of thousands of "laws" that govern every moment of wakefulness. The observance of the Sabbath involves a large body of law. Almost all well-known Jews who practiced individual seclusion still returned home for the Sabbath to be with their families. The Sabbath itself is like a retreat for anyone who observes it seriously. It has a completely different set of purification practices from the other days of the week and a large number of rules that people not accustomed to such detailed observance often find frustrating. These complex laws are designed to distinguish between the holy and profane, the pure and impure.

These examples show the broad sweep of purification practices and suggest principles we can observe when setting up a personal retreat. Some of us may choose to follow a traditional path that has a clear set of practices; others will select particular practices for the period of the retreat. During a retreat, we come to realize a symbiotic relationship between practice and purification. We will see that the integrity with which we approach a practice magnifies its purifying qualities, and this in turn strengthens the practice itself.

On retreat we often resolve to improve our lives outside the retreat setting. This is a natural part of the transformation process, to "clean up our act," as a part of the continuous opening of the heart. The more we keep our lives well ordered in day-to-day activities, the greater will be the reward during our periods of solitude. The more powerful our experience on retreat, the better our lives will function. The process works as a great power reactor, building to a critical mass, until there is a major breakthrough. Then we will reach a new plateau, build another foundation, and begin the process again.

In *Autobiography of a Yogi*, Paramahansa Yogananda wrote:

> Brother Lawrence, the 17th-century Christian mystic, tells us his first glimpse of God-realization came about by viewing a tree. Nearly all human beings have seen a tree; few, alas, have thereby seen the tree's Creator. . . . Yet the ordinary man is not therefore shut out from the possibility of divine communion. He needs, for soul recollection, no more than the kriya yoga technique [a method of directing the consciousness inward in meditation], a daily observance of the moral precepts, and an ability to cry sincerely: "Lord, I yearn to know Thee!"[9]

In a footnote, he added:

> The "ordinary man" must make a spiritual start somewhere, sometime. "The journey of a thousand miles begins with one step," Lao-tzu observed. According to Lord Buddha: "Let no man think lightly of good, saying in his heart, 'It will not come to me.' By the falling of waterdrops a pot is filled; the wise man becomes full of good, even if he gather it little by little."[10]

THE FOUNDATION OF SPIRITUAL PRACTICE

Begin with a little. It may not seem like much, but one practice leads to another. The principles for selecting retreat practices are not complex. They should be something we actually, physically do, something in the world of action. They should not be too distracting or too demanding on our retreat time. Many small actions spread throughout the day are better than one long one. The practices should not be complicated and should be a change from our normal routine; if the action is too natural, it loses a sense of practice.

In choosing a practice, we need to ask ourselves: "Might this harm anyone or anything? Does it have a quality of surrender or sacrifice?" Do we sense a spiritual quality—are we comfortable with it?

When beginning an independent retreat, we often consider practices in each of the following areas: sleep, food, clothing, cleanliness, exercise, and physical environment.

Some suggestions in the area of sleep are to change the bed to a thinner or narrower mat, sleep on the ground, get up earlier, or change our sleeping habits in some other way. Regarding food, we may change diet, eliminate certain items like sugar, go on a juice fast, eat only raw foods, eat less often, or follow a vegetarian or vegan diet. We could select any one or a combination of these practices.

In clothing we have potential for ritual—wearing something special, or something with its own history. Some people associate a retreat with a certain article of clothing and after a while the simple act of putting it on affects consciousness. For cleanliness, we can make a ritual out of washing the body, washing more carefully, caring for body parts in order, or visualizing our burdens being washed away and the light shining through. I know someone who places her feet near the drain at the end of the bath and as the water flows out, visualizes all her negativity flowing out of the heels and vanishing with the water.

Exercise is important on retreat because we are much more sedentary than usual and need to stretch. Practices like yoga or t'ai chi chuan are both meditative and purifying, and there are many other forms of exercise. A simple routine of warm-up and stretching can be done a few times a day in a thoughtful way that incorporates a sense of surrender.

A practice could also be developed of relating to the physical environment of the retreat space. It may be keeping things tidy and in place, or a careful cleanup a few times a day. A useful practice, for example, is never to leave dishes to clean, articles to pick up, or the bed unmade. This is a practice of leaving no tracks; in essence, being invisible.

These are simple tasks to do. They are steps on the path of building virtue. As retreats become longer, and more experience is gained, we build on these practices and find that they overflow into daily life. This is a way to integrate a retreat with normal daily activities—ultimately every retreatant's goal. The idea of purification slowly penetrates until we discover each action has a potential to cleanse the inner being both in the way it is approached and the way it manifests. This is why virtue remains a keystone in every spiritual practice.

# CONCENTRATION

Concentration is the hub, the center of all meditation practice. Purity is perhaps the axle. If the axle is uneven, rusted, bent, or not strong enough, the hub can barely function. We work on purity to strengthen this focal point, and then we direct our attention to our concentration.

If a wheel has a distorted hub, it cannot stay on track. Every meditation practice works to build the power of concentration. The first realization a meditator needs to acquire is the understanding that concentration skills can be improved. When people say "I have a bad memory" or "I have poor concentration," they are nurturing a disempowering belief. Memory and concentration are not static qualities but skills that can be improved constantly.

It may be true that the aging process introduces some degeneration of these skills, but many elderly sages had memory or concentration abilities far beyond the average twenty-year-old today. Moreover, almost everyone can accomplish the one-pointedness that is the hallmark of advanced meditation.

Our first task is to affirm that we can develop concentration despite our initial experiences of wildly spinning minds when we sit in meditation. Our affirmation will be strengthened by the insight we gain in our practice that we really do not have to be distracted while we are meditating.

As beginning meditators, our minds grasp at every stimulus. Even something as insignificant as the sound of a scratch or a pin dropping is enough to disturb novice meditators. We begin to make associations with the sound, and we get caught up with anything related to it. Perhaps we simply react negatively, pushing it away, becoming angry with it.

After a while, we begin to realize that sounds of one kind or another are always going to be present. Some will be more annoying than others. Then we will realize that even normally bothersome sounds are not always distracting; they irritate us merely some of the time.

Our problem is not the sound but the mind that is distracting itself. Our minds become agitated by trying to grasp sounds, chasing after them, or by trying to push them away. When our minds are not bothered, we hardly notice most sounds. In fact, our daily life is filled with sound that we do not relate to because we are focused on something else.

At this moment, stop reading just for a few seconds and listen. Stop! Listen! Do you hear those quiet sounds? Little noises in the house or outside? Or noises not so little? Yet while you were reading, you were oblivious to most noticeable sound. This is normal concentration and we all have an ample supply. The mind could not function without these natural filters that allow us to focus on our activities and eliminate extraneous stimuli.

Many people find it relaxing to engage in mental activity, such as doing a crossword puzzle. Their minds are active, searching for words, trying to make letters fit. Indeed, their minds are extremely busy. Why is this so relaxing? Because a person completing a puzzle is focused on one subject—innocuous words—and this minimizes other mental activities. Our spontaneous concentration screens out distractions.

The next level of insight is the realization that just as sound, light, and movement are not intrinsic disturbances, and our concentration can mute or eliminate them from our consciousness, it follows that initial thought forms do not have to disturb us. The reader should distinguish between initial thoughts that arise spontaneously as compared with associative thinking that is a matrix of connected thoughts. In this instance, we are concerned with spontaneous individual thoughts that continually arise.

The rapid-fire workings of our minds make it difficult to observe the inception of thought. There are many theories concerning the mechanism of thinking, but somewhere along the way a thought enters consciousness. Once this happens, the mind tends to bring in a stream of associations that link one thought with another into ideas and concepts.

Near the beginning of any thought process, during the initial moments of blossoming or early in the stream of associations, we can release the thought form. This "letting-go" process is precisely the same as when we *choose to ignore* a potential distraction of an outside stimulus, like a sound, and instantly release it from our consciousness. This powerful insight leads to a major plateau in the enlightenment process—releasing thoughts as they arise—but it takes time and effort to master.

What causes thoughts to arise? This is a major conundrum of science as well as spirituality. Some scientists believe that a large percentage of thought is spontaneous and unpredictable. There may be causal factors, but these are indeterminate. For example, what makes a bird chirp at a particular moment? Science has not yet developed a way to predict the precise moment a bird will chirp, a limb will break, or lightning will strike.

In the past, scientists sometimes postulated that such happenings were ultimately predictable because every cause has an effect and every effect a cause. Theoretically, they asserted, if a computer could calculate all the variables, we would understand that responses like chirping, breaking limbs, or lightning are predictable. It is true that the number of variables is enormous and no known computer is large enough to manage all the data. But, according to traditional science, it will eventually be possible to predict every action that has a cause.

Yet modern science is at the cutting edge between the traditional approach and intuitive understanding. Today's scientists say the number of variables is infinite and there could *never* be a method of prediction—spontaneity is a fact of life. Moreover, they add, the mechanistic theory of direct causality may be incomplete. The future may bring proof that some variables do not fit causal patterns as we know them, and then even with an "infinite" computer, the instant of action would always remain unpredictable.

In the last few decades science has begun to entertain ideas that mystics have been describing for thousands of years, such as the position that most of our thought processes are unpredictable. Some thoughts are clearly activated by external stimuli, and they lend themselves to causal analysis. But others seem to appear on their own.

Our normal relationship to a thought initially is to grasp it, associate with it, and turn it into concepts, ideas, mental inventions. Each new thought opens us to new universes. This stream of internal universes is the personal world we live in. Each conjured universe affects our emotions and our interactions with everything around us.

Just as our concentration is higher when we are reading and background sounds are not so disturbing, so we can use concentration to minimize the birthing of these inner universes. We can train ourselves to listen more carefully for external sounds while reading. For example, put your attention into your listening center right now, this moment, while you are reading. You can hear sounds, but they still remain as background sounds; they come and go without your mind grasping at them. Your mind hears these sounds, but it is engaged in reading. So too with thoughts. They can come and go without becoming distinct internal worlds, without your being attracted to them, as long as you are concentrating.

During meditation, our concentration naturally intensifies. Sounds which were imperceptible before suddenly become apparent. Distant, subtle sounds can become a distinct part of the environment. On one retreat, after four weeks of silence, I was lying on my back, resting, when I suddenly realized I was listening to a loud waterfall, crashing all around me. It was so loud, I was certain I was dreaming or hallucinating. It did not go away, even when I stood up and walked around.

This waterfall sound continued for days. I had no idea what it could be, but it seemed louder when I lay on the ground. After a few days, I understood. It was indeed a waterfall. Far under the ground little rivulets and streams of water were dripping through the porous rock, millions of drops moving underground. This was my waterfall. Now I know why the well dug at that site produced the best water flow for miles around. The well hit water at 102 feet.

After a fifty-day solitary practice one meditator recorded the following:

> During the course of the practice the hallucinations gradually diminished, my concentration deepened, and eventually I came to experience continuous samādhi. All my senses became clearer and sharper, including my smell and hearing, to the point that I felt I could hear the sound of incense burning—an experience recorded in Mikkyō [esoteric Buddhism] texts.[11]

We hear, see, and feel in an entirely new way on retreat. We become more sensitized; our filters drop away. So too with our thoughts. Nothing new really happens. Normally, we are so busily engaged in life that most of our internal activity flows past unnoticed like a vast underground river. When we limit the all-consuming, everyday demands on our consciousness, our natural concentration and ability to focus is heightened, and we tend to pay more attention to sound, light, and movement.

Gradually, we are able to notice ongoing stimuli without trying to grasp them. They rise and fall on their own. As we observe these natural phenomena, we begin to appreciate that the same is true of thought processes. We become skilled in noticing how our thoughts constantly rise and fall. The more we are able to relinquish our desire to grasp and chase after our thoughts, the keener our awareness.

Our concentration is strongest when we are engaged in something that interests us. Our difficulty in concentrating is not so much an innate weakness as it is a function of interest.

A great many concentration practices exist. The power

derived from meditation is dependent upon our strength of concentration. If we study the literature of enlightenment, we will discover that almost every established meditation practice can be a path of liberation if we have strong concentration skills.

These practices fall into basic categories: visualization, mantra, body awareness, ritual or controlled movement, and intense focus on an object. A concentration practice may mix categories and there may be practices that extend beyond these definitions. For the most part, however, these groupings cover the majority of established meditation practices.

The definition of concentration covers a wide range and has many nuances. A generally accepted idea is "one-pointedness," like a magnifying glass focusing the sun's rays into one intense spot. Another aspect is the polar opposite of one-pointedness: diffusion. This is a wide-sweeping awareness of everything happening in that moment. The archetype of the samurai is one who is a master of diffusion concentration. He is aware of everything; nothing goes unnoticed. It is said that the Buddha could distinguish seventy trillion variables in each moment.

Yet another definition of concentration transcends the basic psychological theory of ground and figure. The ground is like a backdrop to a scene, while the figure is the object in front of the backdrop. Right now, the figure for you is these words and the book you are holding; the ground is everything else happening around you while you are reading. Although much concentration theory is related to the figure—that is, you can have one-pointed concentration on the words you are reading, and the diffusion theory of concentration is directed to the backdrop—there is a third idea of concentration: the concept of the guru.

Guru concentration is transcendental. It is a super-awareness, a conscious experience of being in the presence of a perfectly illuminated entity who is aware of everything that is happening, and is bringing profound insight to this awareness. In essence, guru concentration is as though one is relating to consciousness through the mind of another. This type of practice is found in the Hindu tradition with which we identify gurus, as well as in meditation practices that focus on Jesus and the Christian saints, Muhammad and the Sufi saints, the Jewish patriarchs, matriarchs, and rebbes, or Buddha and the *bodhisattvas*.

The word *guru* itself can be interpreted (according to Ramana Maharshi) as a form of the Sanskrit word *guri,* which means concentration.[12] One aspect of a living guru, of course, is to be a guide and teacher. However, this other, transcendental aspect, can be accomplished even if the guru is no longer living. The guru's presence permeates every thought and action of the practitioner. In essence, the practitioner dwells in the presence of the guru to such an extent that any sense of personal identity dissolves, and the disciple becomes merely a vehicle through which the guru ideal is represented. Simply expressed, we experience everything through the eyes, ears, and senses of the guru—we no longer have a "self"-identity.

Thus concentration is of three kinds: highly focused, highly diffused, or dwelling in the continuous presence of the guru. Each kind has techniques that will strengthen it. The beginning meditator will encounter a variety of practices, the effectiveness of which will depend upon his or her state of mind at the time as well as the environment in which the practice is undertaken.

It is usually advantageous to begin with less compli-cated concentration practices that are easy to explain, so we can begin straight away. Being constantly aware of our breath or focusing intently on a flame are such practices as compared with complex systems, such as practicing Japanese tea ceremony or learning t'ai chi chuan. Yet, even the most basic concentration practices are difficult. Many spiritual disciplines begin with single-focus practices, move to more complex areas, and then return to the simple practices when the meditator is well advanced on the path. It is always possible to refine our concentration by using the most basic exercises.

The most common practice is the simplest one—observing our breath entering and leaving the body. That is all. There are no images to remember, no mantras to sound, no movements. It can be done anywhere at any time because we are all familiar with this constant of life: breath. Therefore, breath is an ideal focus for developing concentration. (For a description of different breathing exercises, see the chapter on breath in my earlier book, *Silence, Simplicity, and Solitude*.)

As with all practices, concentration is not an end in itself. The Venerable Ajahn Chah, a Buddhist teacher in Thailand who was the guide for a number of contemporary Vipassanā teachers in the West, said:

> If you're sitting just to get concentrated so you can feel happy and pleasant, you're wasting your time. The practice is to sit and let your heart become still and concentrated and then to use that concentration to examine the nature of the mind and body. Otherwise, if you simply make the heart/mind quiet, it will be peaceful and free of defilement only as long as you sit. This is like using a stone to cover a garbage pit; when you take away the stone, the pit is still infested and full of garbage.[13]

All forms of yoga in the Hindu tradition have a fundamental element of concentration at the center of the practice, despite the fact that the emphasis of yogic discipline covers a wide variety of expression, including emotional (*bhakti* or tantric yoga), intellectual (*jñāna* or *rāja* yoga), and physical (*hatha* or *karma* yoga). Judaism, on the other hand, has a definite accent on the intellectual side, the aspect of *jñāna* yoga, the path of knowledge.

The primary concentration practice in Judaism is "Talmud Torah," an intense study of Talmud (a complex compilation of religious law based on Biblical exegesis), which is pursued from early morning until late at night, for many years, or even a lifetime. This all-important Jewish practice is the keystone of spiritual discipline, and many Jewish sages claim that the study of Torah leads to ever higher stages of enlightenment, beginning with greater precision in thinking, which leads to deeper commitment, and ridding oneself of negative traits. This is followed by restraint in frivolous actions, then higher levels of purification that eliminate all desire to engage in spiritually injurious actions. This in turn leads to humility and the deep understanding of the implications of sin. Then comes saintliness, enlightenment, and finally life eternal.[14]

The Western approach to concentration can be illuminated by a verse in Proverbs, said to be composed by King Solomon, the wisest man of his time:

> I passed by the field of a lazy man, and by the vineyard of a man who does not pay attention, and behold, all of it was grown over with thorns, and covered with nettles and its stone wall had fallen. And I saw and considered it, I saw and took instruction. A little sleep, a little slumber, a little folding of the hands to sleep—and poverty comes upon you like a marauder, and your desires like an armed man.[15]

One interpretation of this verse is that if we do not engage in regular study, building concentration and mindfulness, then our mind will become overgrown with thorns and nettles, and its foundations will collapse.

Eventually we will become vulnerable to impoverished thought and uncontrollable desire. As a result, unconscious and spiritually destructive decisions will be made, leading in an ever-spiraling downward path.[16]

Traditional meditation practice both East and West is in accord on this point. Without concentration, the mind is like an unbridled wild horse, keeping our lives in chaos, leading us into terrible predicaments. When the reins of concentration are loose, we flail in all directions and bring great suffering to ourselves. In the beginning these reins are hard to seize. With effort, however, we can get a grip on them and ultimately tighten them.

The wild horse's nature will not change—even when it is reined in, we must be firm. As our attention strengthens, we reach a deeper understanding of life. Then the horse becomes our best friend. Human beings have an unparalleled potential for enlightenment and awareness. The mind as a wild horse is our enemy, but the trained, highly concentrated mind is our greatest gift.

Our perverse nature would have us believe that life is better, more enjoyable, and easier when the horse is running free. However, when we are caught in a jumble of emotions, depression, or a sense of helplessness and despair, we are unable to see that our condition is accentuated by our undisciplined minds. The skills of concentration open the gates of insight, and the whole pattern becomes obvious.

There is usually great internal resistance to developing a regular practice for building concentration. The mind has a wide variety of tricks, some of which are recognizable right away, and others so subtle it comes as a shock when they are discovered. The key to success in strengthening concentration is continuous practice, and the key to developing continuous practice is called *effort*.

# EFFORT

The use of effort on the spiritual path is an enigma for the aspirant, particularly a Westerner who equates effort with striving—trying to do something, using energy to make something happen. It is natural to believe that some kind of effort is necessary in order to accomplish anything, yet we are often cautioned by spiritual masters that striving is self-defeating and keeps us from our aspirations.

This paradox was neatly summed up by a third-century Sufi, Abu Said al-Kharraz, who said:

> *He who believes that he can reach God by his exertions hurls himself into an endless torment; and he who believes that he can reach Him without exertions, hurls himself into an endless wishful dream.*[17]

How can we have effort without effort? One solution is to analyze what is behind effort. If there is someone (a sense of oneself) making an effort, that someone is likely to run into trouble. But if the effort is merely being channeled and there is no ego attachment, then a person will not be a victim of his or her own failed expectations.

"Egoless" effort is not without exertion. Traditional Sufi practices, for example, can be strenuous and have included hanging upside down in a dark well, the constant repetition of God's name, and being confined in a cave for

THE FOUNDATION OF SPIRITUAL PRACTICE

forty days without any sensory input. A thousand years ago, the Sufis invented their own versions of isolation chambers.

Yet, another Sufi teacher, Bāyezīd Bistāmī (ninth century) saw things differently:

> I have never seen anything come of ritual prayer but the upright posture of the body, or of fasting anything but hunger. All that I have comes from His grace, not from my action. A man can produce nothing by exertion and activity. . . . The happy man is he whose foot, as he walks along, stumbles suddenly on a treasure so that he grows rich.[18]

We are left with a new paradox: We can attain nothing by exertion yet we must not let up in our spiritual aspirations. Bistāmī clarifies this a little for us: "One must do everything in spiritual struggle, but [in success] one must see the grace of God and not one's own act." Spiritual effort must be without the sense of an "I" performing the act; the process is simply the fulfilling of divine will. The question is: How do we develop this "egoless" effort?

A Zen story sheds some light on the matter. A well-known swordsman had a son named Matajuro who did not seem to have any talent with a sword. Rather than lose face by acknowledging that his son was inept, the father disowned him. Matajuro sought out a famous sword master named Banzo, only to be told that he did not meet the requirements.

> "But if I work hard, how many years will it take me to become a master?" asked Matajuro.
> "The rest of your life," replied Banzo.
> "I cannot wait that long," explained Matajuro. "I am willing to pass through any hardship if only you will teach me. If I become your devoted servant, how long might it be?"

*"Oh, maybe ten years," Banzo relented.*

*"My father is getting old, and soon I must take care of him,"* continued Matajuro. *"If I work far more intensively, how long would it take me?"*

*"Oh, maybe thirty years," said Banzo.*

*"Why is that?" asked Matajuro. "First you say ten and now thirty years. I will undergo any hardship to master this art in the shortest time!"*

*"Well," said Banzo, "in that case you will have to remain with me for seventy years. A man in such a hurry as you are to get results seldom learns quickly."*

*"Very well," declared the youth, understanding at last that he was being rebuked for impatience, "I agree."*[19]

The story describes how Matajuro was not allowed to speak of fencing or touch a sword. He did the cooking and the dishes, made the beds, cleaned the yard, and cared for the garden.

After three years Matajuro became sad because he had not even started working with a sword. Then one day Banzo quietly entered the room and whacked him with a wooden sword. The following day Banzo again attacked him by surprise and clouted him with a blunt sword.

After that, at every moment, Matajuro had to be aware of sudden assaults. The anticipation of Banzo's sword caused an alertness and awareness that gave him a high degree of precision. As a result, he quickly learned the art of swordsmanship. It is said that "Matajuro became the greatest swordsman in the land."[20]

The effort needed in spiritual work is not anything like the normal effort we make in our daily living. It requires acute attention on a level that transcends self-awareness. The first step toward this effort is complete self-effacement. The next step is total absorption in the focus of our concentration. This level of absorption may also be viewed as the ability to sustain a continuous level of attention. Clearly, it is not easy to achieve this state of mind.

A Zen lesson given by the contemporary Yasutani-roshi uses a metaphor of swordsmanship to describe spiritual effort. He describes the practice of *shikan-taza,* which literally means "nothing but sitting." There is no *kōan,* no counting the breath, nothing extraneous on which to concentrate—just sitting. This type of meditation requires intense awareness. Yasutani-roshi says:

> Shikan-taza *is a heightened state of concentrated awareness wherein one is neither tense nor hurried, and certainly never slack. It is the mind of somebody facing death. Let us imagine that you are engaged in a duel of swordsmanship of the kind that used to take place in ancient Japan. As you face your opponent you are unceasingly watchful, set, ready. Were you to relax your vigilance even momentarily, you would be cut down instantly. A crowd gathers to see the fight. Since you are not blind you see them from the corner of your eye, and since you are not deaf you hear them. But not for an instant is your mind captured by these sense impressions.*[21]

Although one is not in a tense or hurried state in *shikan-taza* meditation, in the beginning it is advisable not to attempt it for more than half an hour at a time, for it takes a great deal of effort. The effort entails becoming fully aware of whatever is going on without reacting to it. The student is required to abandon the natural inclination to follow sensory input, to glance away, or become distracted even for a moment by a peripheral sound, sight, or thought. This "not-doing" what we normally do, "not-thinking" the way we normally think, demands tremendous effort and discipline.

Yasutani-roshi goes on to say:

> Compared with an unskilled swordsman, a master uses his sword effortlessly. But this was not always the case, for there was a time

*when he had to strain himself to the utmost, owing to imperfect technique, to preserve his life. It is no different with* shikan-taza. *In the beginning tension is unavoidable, but with experience this tense* zazen *ripens into relaxed yet fully attentive sitting. . . . But do not for one minute imagine that such sitting can be achieved without long and dedicated practice.*[22]

In spiritual terminology, effort is related to attentiveness. The total composite of our attention is sometimes called the "mind's eye." We all have a natural power to focus sharply, particularly in special situations, such as life-threatening moments, or deeply emotional events. The mind's eye opens wide at these times and we remember them vividly for the rest of our lives.

The quality of the times when we are naturally attentive is that these moments are especially *interesting* to us. When we are deeply interested in something, we are attentive without effort. This kind of interest transcends the ego in the sense of self-identification. It operates just on the primal levels, such as pure survival. Thus, interest is the fundamental ingredient of egoless effort.

This is the secret of Banzo's teaching. The first period of Matajuro's training was in self-effacement. He had to let go of his attachment to becoming a great swordsman. Then, the whole method of instruction was directed to raising pure, undiluted interest. This also is the teaching of Yasutani-roshi. When a swordsman is facing instant death, his attentiveness is perfect, his interest is unwavering.

Interest in becoming enlightened is not enough. It is an abstraction and the interest is invariably ego-centered; this kind of interest springs from desire and grasping. The interest level that is a foundation for effort has more the nature of an imperative.

We do not choose to be interested when facing death. It is an instant response; it sweeps us away. The kind of interest important here does not involve will; there is no decision process. It is a genuine, involuntary interest that captures us and holds us tightly in its grip. It has an instinctual aspect in that it transcends ego-awareness; there is no sense of "I/me" when dwelling in the sphere of this intense interest. It may be sustained for a moment or it can continue for a long period. Indeed, Banzo's method was to imprint this interest as a moment-to-moment approach to life. The sign of a true master is that his or her absorption never wavers; the master remains attentive at all times.

The paradox regarding effort is related to the differentiation of the interest that is its driving force. When our interest is willful, we are driven by ego and desire. When our interest is involuntary and authentic—an overwhelming imperative—it leads to the true effortlessness of complete attention. This is the "choiceless awareness" Krishnamurti discusses. He tells us, "Just do it!" No decisions, no conjectures, no thoughts; we simply accept eternal wisdom teachings and follow them.

This is one of those deceptively simple teachings that remains extraordinarily difficult. How do we do something without deciding to do it? We know that we do not *decide* to pay attention when somebody is pointing a gun at our heads. We just do it. No hesitation. Our primal interest in the event effortlessly rivets us.

How do we develop the spontaneous interest that will result in choiceless awareness? The answer, as is often the case, lies in the question. Choice, Krishnamurti points out, implies confusion. Where there is no confusion, there is no choice; and, vice versa, where there is no choice, no confusion. When we relinquish the notion of choice, there is surrender.

Sri Ramana Maharshi suggests:

*There are only two ways to conquer destiny or be independent of it. One is to enquire for whom is this destiny and discover that only the ego is bound by destiny and not the Self, and that the ego is nonexistent. The other way is to kill the ego by completely surrendering to the Lord, by realising one's helplessness and saying all the time, "Not I but thou, O Lord," giving up all sense of "I" and "mine" and leaving it to the Lord to do what he likes with you. Surrender can never be regarded as complete as long as the devotee wants this or that from the Lord. True surrender is love of God for the sake of love and nothing else, not even for the sake of liberation. In other words, complete effacement of the ego is necessary to conquer destiny, whether you achieve this effacement through self-enquiry or through* bhakti marga *(the way of devotion).*[23]

When we consider the idea of surrender, using the metaphor of a battlefield, we find two aspects: The time prior to the surrender and the time following it. Prior to surrender we envision a great struggle, a conflict that continues until the resources of one side are depleted. After surrender, we experience no struggle at all, it is over. In other words, leading up to surrender is a period of effort, following a surrender there is no effort.

The battlefield metaphor has implications that the losers are enslaved by the winners. They may be abused and exploited. Nobody wants to be on the losing side.

In many ways the fear of surrender on the spiritual battleground has similar connotations. Surrender implies giving in, losing our identities, not having anything as a result. As long as we have our "selves," we experience a feeling of power, a sense of identity. Without this sense of self, we imagine that we would be defenseless.

Most of us, therefore, choose to continue the battle, holding on to our identity at all costs. We maintain an illusion of constant conflict, the "me" opposed to the "not-me." As soon as we admit the possibility of a new perspective, we realize that both the "me" and the "not-me" are inventions. It turns out not to be a battle at all, but a series of shields, each reflecting the other side in an infinite regression, blocking the true experience that rests behind these shields. Once the shields are surrendered, the field is transformed from conflict to peace, and our inner world becomes an exquisite garden filled with the beauty of creation.

In each tradition, one surrenders to its highest ideal. In the West, surrender is to the God of Abraham, the one and only Creator of the universe. In Hinduism surrender is to Brahman, in Buddhism to the Buddha essence in all creation, in Taoism to the Way.

In *The Varieties of Religious Experience,* William James has a description that can serve as an archetype for the conversion that takes place through surrender. He begins the discussion by pointing out that one way to deal with anger, worry, fear, and despair is to become so exhausted in the struggle that "we drop down, give up, and *don't care* any longer." This is obvious surrender. He then says:

> So long as the egoistic worry of the sick soul guards the door, the expansive confidence of the soul of faith gains no presence. But let the former faint away, even but for a moment, and the latter can profit by the opportunity, and, having once acquired possession, may retain it. Carlyle's Teufelsdrockh [*the main character of Thomas Carlyle's classic* Sartor Resartus[24]] *passes from the everlasting No to the everlasting Yes through a "Center of Indifference."*[25]

This is a splendid encapsulation of the process. The everlasting No represents the time that precedes surrender, as we struggle, constantly grasping for an identity. The Center of Indifference is the state of surrender, the place we must attain in order to transform this continuous No into the everlasting Yes, the affirmation that accompanies awareness and universal truth.

James then goes on to cite many testimonies of "conversion," which is the code word for the Christian enlightenment experience. It should not be confused with the idea of converting from one tradition to another. Rather, it is the internal conversion a person experiences at a supreme moment of awareness. Prior to this moment, the person may feel that all prayers remain unanswered. After conversion, the person experiences the light of everlasting divine presence. Time and again in these accounts, we observe a dark period of emptiness, a letting go and surrender of the self, and then a new awareness of infinite light.

The following is a typical account from someone who had been a habitual drinker:

> About midday I made on my knees the first prayer before God for twenty years. I did not ask to be forgiven; I felt that was no good, for I would be sure to fall again. Well, what did I do? I committed myself to Him in the profoundest belief that my individuality was going to be destroyed, that He would take all from me, and I was willing. In such a surrender lies the secret of a holy life. From that hour drink has had no terrors for me: I never touch it, never want it. . . . Since I gave up to God all ownership in my own life, He has guided me in a thousand ways, and has opened my path in a way almost incredible to those who do not enjoy the blessing of a truly surrendered life.[26]

Surrender opens the gates of choiceless awareness. Once this occurs, nothing distracts our attentiveness from the task at hand. Anything can become spontaneously interesting. This is how our efforts become effortless.

Spontaneous interest occurs only when we transcend the continuous self-engagement that is our normal daily pattern. Most of our time is spent in relating everything to the self—comparing, judging, reviewing the past, or planning for the future; all these are functions of continuous engagement in maintaining self-identity. The moments of total attention occur when a primal event pushes away this constant reinforcement of the self.

The process of surrender inhibits self-indulgence, and the result is greater opportunity for spontaneous interest and attentiveness, which lead to a state of absorption. We can be deeply captivated by anything—our breath, an ant walking across the ground, the wind in the leaves. Absorption is the hallmark of the release of ego-identification and this inevitably leads to a universe of expanded awareness.

This helps to clarify our paradox somewhat. The effort made by a spiritual aspirant is not so much directed toward the practice as toward surrender itself. Surrender takes considerable effort throughout the spiritual process, especially in the early stages. This ultimately yields an effortless practice—practice for its own sake, without any goal orientation.

We exert ourselves in the process of surrendering in order to perform our practice without any expectation and without believing that we are doing anything special. Easier said than done, this is a critical prerequisite for successful practice, along with purification and concentration.

Mastery is the last of the four elements of spiritual endeavor. This is a quality related to but distinct from purification, concentration, and effort. It too has its aspect of surrender, and it reveals still another fundamental paradox of the spiritual quest.

# MASTERY

In all ventures, occupations, and vocations we encounter outstanding masters. A musician may become a master, an Olympic athlete is a master of her or his specialty, there are master craftsmen, and we often speak of spiritual masters. The word *master* has a double connotation. It means to be in a superior capacity, which is sometimes taken to mean one person ruling over another. We also understand it to mean gaining superb skills in a particular effort, or knowing something thoroughly.

Spiritual mastery is a combination of both these meanings. We gain power over ourselves and we achieve extraordinary skills and deep understanding. Upon closer inspection, we will find that masters in every field have a dimension of spiritual mastery. The mark of a master is that he or she dwells at the outer limits, transcending the average, often even the superior. In order to achieve this, the master must be disciplined in using the basic principles of practice we have already outlined: purification, concentration, and effort.

When we reflect upon our heroes, we tend to focus on their determination. We envision the musician who practiced ten hours a day from the age of six, the athlete who spent each day in long hours of strenuous workout, the craftsman who worked at his trade steadily for twenty years. In addition to determination, we recognize the necessity of inclination and talent.

Inclination, or motive force, is required in any success story. It is the fuel without which even a perfect engine cannot function. Inclination does not mean wanting to achieve something, but is a force of will without desire. We are moved to do something just for the sake of doing it.

Often in the early stages of mastery there is no specific goal and the student is sustained by the pure balance and harmony of practice. Arduous labor by a budding artisan, physical exercise to the point of exhaustion, or long hours playing a violin or piano are usually motivated by personal inclination. Ambition comes later. In the beginning, however, the idea of fame and fortune is not sufficient to maintain the necessary perseverance. Despite the fact that young people originally undertake a discipline in order to gain approval, their ego needs are usually overpowered by the tediousness of constant effort. When that happens, most people give up a practice, but the potential master will continue. The person who persists over the long term is sustained by this enigmatic quality of inclination.

Talent is another mysterious attribute. We can observe talent when it is expressed, but we cannot assess the nature of talent, where it comes from, why some have it and not others. Each of us discovers activities for which we have natural talent. The skills required to complete a task come to us effortlessly. Other people stumble and are awkward when attempting the same project. We accept our gift without question and wonder why others have a problem. Then we experience the reverse—we are all thumbs, constantly failing in a task, while others seem to be performing it without difficulty.

Although some people possess outstanding talent, it is

not sufficient in itself to assure success. Most masters have indicated that determination and effort were responsible for ninety percent of their success, while talent played a minor role. In fact, when extremely talented individuals lack determination, the most likely result is that others with less talent but more commitment will surpass them.

The way we develop our determination is through gaining power over ourselves. This idea leads to a common paradox in spiritual practice concerning self-identification. Many traditions speak of self-annihilation or letting go of the self-image. Others refer to the yearning self, the attachment of self to the divine. Still others talk of the Self with a capital S, the embodiment of all selves. Some compare the idea of self with that of soul, asserting the existence of a soul, while others say there is no soul.

These descriptions are not only contradictory, they lead to a fundamental paradox. If we have no self, what is the "it" that is attached? If we have no soul, what is it that recognizes that "I" and "me" do not exist? Who is asking? What is behind the who? Moreover, if there is an annihilation, what does the annihilating? This set of face-to-face mirrors reflects back and forth in an infinite query: Who is behind the who? It presents the paradox that all spiritual practice is directed in some way to separating out the *identity* of oneself (which all agree is an illusion), from the essence of this form called "I/me"— but if there is nothing to separate from, what initiates the separating; moreover, how can we even discuss the idea of separation, which implies a duality?

Thus, when we discuss the need for determination, we enter the jaws of the paradox because determination implies a strong sense of "I/me." Otherwise, what would be the aspect so determined to accomplish something? One way to avoid this pitfall is to find a word to express determination without the association of ego. This can be done by discussing an attribute upon which determination is built, the power of restraint.

First we must observe how restraint is at the core of determination. When the young artist practices for long hours, despite the fact that he or she may be inclined to do so, there remain the normal distractions we all experience: wanting to spend time with friends, rest, go for a snack, take the day off, or try something new. Innumerable desires and aversions impinge on us and this young artist all the time.

The master learns how to say "NO!" Each time a desire rises to pull us away from the practice, the answer is "Not now." When an aversion arises to cloud our practice, we say, "Not now." After a while, it does not exist anymore. All traces of an obsessive thought can disappear in just a few minutes, and we may not even be able to remember what it was that just commanded our complete attention.

We see here that the kind of determination needed for mastery is not based on the qualities we normally associate with someone having a drive for success, such as aggressiveness, boldness, or daring. It has more the qualities of steadfastness, tenacity, and fortitude. We might say that the former qualities require active determination, while the latter require passive determination.

Restraint is in the category of passive determination. Obviously, our egos play a role in self-restraint, but there is a clear differentiation between trying to achieve something, which is the goal of active determination, and separating ourselves from distraction, which is the immediate result of passive determination. Indeed, while the desire to achieve something enhances ego–identification, restraint is the key that helps us gain distance and objectivity upon self-reflection.

Through restraint, the master becomes increasingly familiar with the ephemeral nature of attachments and aversions and thereby tends to identify much less with them. When the self is not identified with these needs, it becomes possible to have an entirely new perspective and relationship with our essential nature. Athletes, for ex- ample, are known to be more accepting of pain than non-athletes. They have much less identification with the pain, and thus they do not have the same degree of aversion non-athletes experience. Indeed, pain and ath- letics go hand in hand. It is a way of life.

All mastery has this quality of diminishing the identi- fication with the self. However, many fields of endeavor compensate and rebuild ego through the rewards of success, fame, and fortune. These may provide marvelous material benefits, but they reduce if not eliminate the spiritual benefits.

The attainment of mastery through restraint is a prin- cipal landmark along the path of self-discovery. Religious traditions are often defined by the body of law they encompass, as well as their ideology. In each tradition, however, many principles of self-restraint do not fit into the category of legal dogma, but have much more the characteristic of spiritual counsel.

Moses Hayim Luzzatto, a medieval Kabbalist, wrote a number of treatises on spiritually "unhealthy" conduct. One of his best known works, *The Path of the Just,* is a detailed description of the process of transformation into the highest spiritual potential. A key step along the way is restraint, which Luzzatto called "withdrawal" (*haprishut*).[27]

### THE FOUNDATION OF SPIRITUAL PRACTICE

*[The process is] withdrawing oneself from something, forbidding to oneself something which is permitted [by Jewish law] . . . the understanding being that a person should withdraw and separate himself from anything which might give rise to something that could bring evil, even though it does not bring it about at the moment and even though it is not evil in itself.*[28]

Luzzatto cites examples of behavior also frowned upon in other traditions: drinking too much wine, eating food until sated, oversleeping, gossiping, sexuality, and day-dreaming. Overindulgence in any activity should be avoided. Everything in the world ultimately poses a spiritual danger and must be approached with care. Even simple talking can be refreshing and worthwhile or can degenerate into gossip, slander, and outright lies.

Luzzatto explains that withdrawal from the world should not be overdone, for excessive restraint itself can become self-indulgent and self-righteous. Still:

*More desirable than anything else in respect to the attainment of [withdrawal] is solitude; for when one removes worldly goods from before his eyes, he removes desire for them from his heart. As [King] David said in praise of solitude, "Who will give me the wings of a dove . . . I would wander far off; I would lie down in the desert." (Psalms 55:7) We find that the Prophets Elijah and Elisha situated themselves in the mountains in keeping with their practice of seclusion; and the Sages, the first saints, of blessed memory, followed in their footsteps, for they found this practice the most effective means of acquiring perfection. . . .*[29]

The very practice of retreat is by definition a form of restraint. We pull ourselves out of the world, mini-mizing the input of stimuli, freeing ourselves from the constant processing of data. The practice of seclusion is the path of insight followed by almost all historical spiritual guides.

Although a retreat is a gross form of restraint, practicing temperance in everything we do leads to much greater control of the mental process. This ultimate ability to "restrain one's thoughts," is known in Sufism as *baz gard,* and is one of the eight principles of practice for Naqshbandiyya Sufis. The ability to restrain thought is the prerequisite for observing the thought process, which itself is a prerequisite for concentrating on God.[30]

Restraint can take a fairly mild form, such as eating, sleeping, or performing any activity less than usual. It can also be more oriented to the thought process, allowing less room for self-indulgence. When the mind calls out with a hunger message, we can ignore the desire and turn our attention to something else. The hunger will soon disappear. Every time the mind complains, supplicates, pleads, prods, or demands, we simply register the message and then continue with whatever we were doing before being interrupted. This reins in the mind and reconditions our internal process by not reacting as we normally do. The more we delay our response to these signals, the less compelling they seem to be. This is the road to mastering inner silence.

In one Buddhist practice, even more aggressiveness is used in restraint. Whatever the mind wants, we do just the opposite:

> When Sariputta was going for alms-food, he saw that greed said, "Give me a lot," so he said, "Give me a little." If defilement says, "Give it to me fast," our Path says, "Give it to me slowly." If attachment wants hot, soft food, then our Path asks for it hard and cold.[31]

Mastery is self-discipline, the ability to say no, as well as the strength to override our impulses and do just the opposite. Restraint is the tool used to ascertain "who is in charge." We may not be able to define the "who," but it is clear that indulging the impulses strengthens ego and the illusory part of the self. This ego aspect certainly does not merit being in charge; indeed this is the distinct feature of our makeup that gets us into so much trouble.

When we are successful in the practice of restraint, the paradoxical nature of "I/me" begins to evaporate, and we gain insight into a different reality. This is achieved by setting arbitrary limits and observing our internal reactions. As we notice thought processes falling into patterns, we gain insight into our nature and our mechanism of self-identification. This is not something easily explained; it must be directly experienced. This is the only way the paradox of self-annihilation can be fathomed.

People expect spiritual masters to have trans-human capabilities, no longer suffering illness, able to perform incredible feats. This is a general misunderstanding. The essence of spiritual mastery lies in the ability to restrain the mind, change its state, and remain in deep concentration without being distracted by normal impulses.

Paramahansa Yogananda points out:

> A sickly body does not indicate that a guru is lacking in divine powers, any more than lifelong health necessarily indicates inner illumination. The distinguishing qualifications of a master are not physical but spiritual. . . . Proof that one is a master, however, is supplied only by the ability to enter at will the breathless state [absorption in superconsciousness] and by the attainment of immutable bliss [union with God].[32]

The perfection of mastery is not, as we might have supposed, a process of achievement. It is much more one of elimination, negation, and restraint. When we pay no attention to distractions, we can proceed on the path. This persistence is the foundation stone of mastery.

In a retreat setting, the opportunity to exercise restraint continually presents itself. This may happen near the end of a scheduled sit. Perhaps the session is supposed to last for forty minutes, but after thirty the mind begins to complain. The more we say no, the more devious the mind becomes to convince us that it is vital to stop before the end of the period. We think, "This is too boring, too stupid, my leg hurts, I'm getting nowhere, this knee will never be the same, I can feel the gangrene coming, they are going to have to cut off my foot."

This is our sense of identity trying to assert itself. Every time we give in, our self-identity is strengthened, ready to cause us even more problems in the future. When self-restraint enters the scene, the mind is quieted. The more self-restraint there is, within limits, the quieter the mind.

Teachers all point out that restraint should be exercised with prudence. Most of us have a tendency to try to move too fast and do too much. This can lead to obsessive and neurotic behavior. Luzzatto sums it up in the following advice:

> What one must be heedful of in the process of acquiring [withdrawal] is not to desire to leap to its farthest reaches in one moment, for he will certainly not be able to make such great strides. He should rather proceed in [withdrawal] little by little, acquiring a little today and adding a little more tomorrow, until he is so habituated to it that it is second nature with him.[33]

Purification, concentration, effort, and mastery are the infrastructure of all spiritual discipline. It is worth reviewing them often when beginning a retreat, whether one is a novice or has thousands of hours' experience. Each principle requires a certain amount of sacrifice, and there are some areas where they overlap. Yet they remain distinct, each significant in its own right, and a meditator or retreatant needs to be intimate with the lesson each has to offer.

# UNPLEASANT
# MIND STATES

# INTRODUCTION

Most of us fill our lives with diversions that constantly preoccupy our minds. When we are not engaged in normal mundane routine, we pack our time with conversations, reading newspapers, watching television, and a multitude of other activities. Rare is the person who is comfortable sitting quietly, doing nothing, allowing time to pass freely.

Even though our daily activities are not particularly demanding and we are able to accomplish them by rote, they still capture our attention sufficiently to influence our awareness. As a result, when people are asked how they are feeling, the answer is usually "fine," even though they may not be. We are uncertain of our mind state or general mood most of the time. It feels neutral.

When we undertake intensive spiritual work, such as a retreat, we try to emancipate ourselves from routine activities and the distractions that cloud our minds. We discover in this process that mind states and moods arise spontaneously and often in great rapidity. In fact, even though we may make a strong effort to develop one-pointed concentration, a constant flow of extraneous thoughts and emotional shifts usually predominates within minutes.

UNPLEASANT MIND STATES

We come to realize that this is the usual state of mind. It is our monkey mind. Most of the time, we do not notice this mind jungle because the majority of our thoughts are fleeting and subtle. Only when they are intense or enduring do thoughts become part of our ordinary consciousness. Often these conscious thoughts are accompanied by emotions such as anger, fear, desire, or aversion, and we act out our lives accordingly.

One of the major benefits of meditation and retreats is that we become more sensitized to these experiences as they arise and are therefore able to minimize the degree to which they overwhelm us. The simple observation that we are in an angry mind state is often sufficient to inhibit it.

This section of the book explores the mind states that trouble us. They often lead to regrettable actions or experiences that might have been avoided. Although we sometimes refer to them as "negative" states, we do not intend to imply that they are "bad." They are negative in the sense that a magnet has a negative and positive polarity. It cannot function without both.

Our normal mental condition is a simple muddle—we usually live in fog. Every so often, we drop out of the fog into another realm. This new mind state becomes our full reality during the period we are in it. The interval may last only a few moments, but at times it goes on for hours, or even days or weeks. When this reality is an unpleasant state, such as anger, fear, pain, or doubt, life can be miserable.

As we learn how to deal with these experiences, we develop tools and techniques to keep them more contained in our everyday lives. This is perhaps the greatest benefit of practices such as intensive retreats. They deepen our spiritual connection with the universe, and give us an entirely new mechanism for coping with the normal ebb and flow of our emotions and thoughts. We gain a wealth of insight when we uncover the true nature of the monkey mind.

# DESIRE

A single-celled blob of protoplasm such as an amoeba has three basic reactions to stimuli: it will be attracted, repelled, or have no response at all. As we move up through the phyla of animal life, we see that all life exhibits these responses: attraction, repulsion, and nothing. Although the human organism is incredibly complex, it shares the same basic response pattern. While the amoeba moves its pseudopod slowly and we can watch its advance or withdrawal, the human process moves at lightning speed and its fundamental nature often becomes hidden in the intricacy of associations. Yet, the principle remains the same. Attraction, which is called desire, and repulsion, which is called aversion, are at the core of most human thought and activity.

Desire is obviously an extremely broad category. It includes natural biological responses such as hunger or thirst, needs for love, shelter, warmth, sex, and the release of body waste; it also extends to the subtler responses related to ego needs for acceptance, self-worth, sense of importance, attractiveness, uniqueness, and any other aspect related to personal identity.

When appetite goes on a rampage, normal hunger turns into gluttony; survival needs may turn into avarice, sexual needs into lust. Ego demands can translate into a wide range of unhealthy states, from cruelty or destructive ambition to mental illness such as paranoia. As desire is by definition related to "I/me," its expression, whether simple or elaborate, always involves isolation. Cravings place boundary lines around us, separating us from everything else. This, according to many spiritual teachers, is the root cause of delusion, pain, and suffering in the world.

Shivapuri Baba, the teacher who reputedly lived to be 137 years old before dying in 1962, had a poetic way of describing the process of original desire transforming into ignorance:

> God has sent Wisdom with you. Wisdom is your friend. Wisdom plays with Desire and by their unlawful contact they gave birth to Mind. This Mind marries a girl named Chapalata or Restlessness and by this he got the five senses. The Mind has got another wife too whose name is Hope and by this second wife he got two sons named Anger and Greed. Thus a family is set up and they make a home to live in this body.
>
> This unlawful playing of Wisdom and Desire is Avidyā or Ignorance. And in course of time, as Mind experiences fears and anxieties through the five senses, he becomes much distracted or disturbed, and then turns back to his mother Wisdom and cries for help. Wisdom then comes and consults YOU, meaning Soul, who then tells her to renounce her family and to remain in communion with YOU or Soul. This communion with Soul is what we call Realization or Bodha.[1]

We find in this brief explanation a profound teaching. Wisdom is our greatest gift, when used properly. Desire, on its own, is an organic part of our makeup. When wisdom and desire get mixed up with each other, our greatest afflictions are born. Shivapuri Baba calls this affliction "Mind," which is clearly a different concept from wisdom. He does not clarify for us exactly what he means by mind, but it has something to do with the intellectualization of sensory input. This cognition keeps us in a state of constant restlessness. A by-product of this union is the clinging nature of the mind which leads to greed and anger.

It is difficult to grasp the true sense of this teaching without experiencing deep meditation or extended retreat. We can sense our restlessness, but we do not really understand the connection between this and normal sensory input. We know that we are sometimes angry and maybe even a little greedy, but we have no idea how prevalent these attributes are in our everyday consciousness, nor do we appreciate the structure of attachment and how it works.

Many people on the spiritual path have labeled desire, clinging, and attachment as negative attributes, the goal being to clear ourselves of these qualities. Often these people fail to realize how easily we can fall into the trap of being attached to non-attachment. Many teachers warn about this, but the mind is so subtle, the trap springs quickly at the slightest nuance. We can often observe teachers who strongly advocate the idea of breaking attachments but who themselves are completely attached to their own methods.

Krishnamurti was explicit on this point:

> The very urge to get rid of desire is still desire, is it not? . . . Recognizing that desire brings conflict, you ask, "How can I be free of desire?" So what you really want is not freedom from desire, but freedom from the worry, the anxiety, the pain which desire causes. . . . As long as there is the desire to gain, to achieve, to become, at whatever level [including the urge to get rid of desire], there is inevitably anxiety, sorrow, fear.[2]

The secret lies not in trying to rid ourselves of desire, clinging, or attachment, but in recognizing the role each plays in our psychological process. This clear recognition and understanding ultimately leads to liberation.

There is a positive role for aspiration. We want to survive, we long for humankind to live in peace and harmony, we yearn to know our true purpose and to be at one with the Divine Source. We have the urge necessary to breathe, cohabit, procreate, be kind, raise healthy children, and even meditate or take a retreat.

It is true that our desire function can be easily corrupted. In an instant it can be turned into an impure craving for personal gain, a longing for ego-oriented achievement, or a sense of becoming somebody special. However, until that point, aspiration is an integral, necessary part of life.

We may think that clinging or attachment are inappropriate qualities for the spiritual aspirant, but many believe these are precisely what is needed to attain the highest levels of personal development. Whether they are appropriate or not depends upon intention and focus.

One of the most important forms of spiritual effort in Judaism is called *devekut*, which is often translated as cleaving, binding, or being attached to God. A large body of Hasidic literature is devoted to this ideal. Gershom Scholem writes about the word *devekut*:

> *This is regarded as the ultimate goal of religious perfection. Devekut can be ecstasy, but its meaning is far more comprehensive. It is a perpetual being-with-God, an intimate union and conformity of the human and divine Will.*[3]

It is interesting to see the counterpoint here between Buddhism, which advocates non-attachment and rejects the Western concept of God, and Judaism, which has as its ultimate goal the spiritual perfection of union with God. These ostensibly diametrically opposed perspectives seem to converge as we explore the peak of perfection in each. A high point of achievement in Buddhism is a state of equanimity (a way of expressing pure non-attachment), which comes from a true understanding of the impermanence of nature and the realization that "all things must pass." In the Jewish perspective, equanimity is also a major stage in the enlightenment process. A Kabbalist named Isaac of Acre (circa 1300) said:

> He who is vouchsafed the entry into the mystery of adhesion to God, devekut, attains to the mystery of equanimity, and he who possesses equanimity attains to loneliness, and from there he comes to the holy Spirit and to prophecy.[4]

How can non-attachment and complete union both result in equanimity? This contradiction was resolved by Rebbe Nachman of Breslov:

> When a person has any desire except to do what God desires, it gives strength to the forces of the Other Side [the evil or dark side]. A man must nullify his own will to the point where he has no will or desire for anything except what God desires. . . .[5]

The distinction here is made between the individual yearning that is in harmony with God's will and that which is not. Where self-identity is mixed with desire, it is the kind of wanting that will inevitably lead to anxiety, sorrow, and fear. Where the resolve is selfless, it would be viewed as being in harmony with God's will. Thus the idea of *devekut* is not so much a cleaving or clinging as it is a melting away, or an absorption of each into the other.

With this understanding, the distinction between *devekut* and the ideal of non-attachment becomes blurred; they are not so different from each other. No self-identity is present in the process of *devekut*, so there is no entity to attach to another. The idea of non-attachment is also focused on the dissolving of self-identity. In the end, the goal of Buddhism is an utter absorption in Buddha Mind, a melting away into what is called the "Unconditioned."

The Sufis discriminate between desire that is justified, *huquq*, or unjustified, *huzuz*:

> Only the unjustified [desires] were combatted, those which exceeded either the limits of the religious law or the measure of pleasure necessary for the preservation of life. [Asked to describe what was meant by the idea of transgression], the Sufi Jalal ud-din-i Rumi [thirteenth century] replied: "When he [a devotee] eats without being hungry."[6]

The focus of all spiritual paths is to eliminate the ambition arising from self-interest, which may be called selfish in its broadest sense. In order to accomplish this, we must first identify the yearning which comes from our pure center of being—longing exclusive of all sense of self—compared with desire tinged even in the slightest way with wanting to gain, achieve, or become something.

When we sit quietly, trying to concentrate on one object, we soon discover that the mind goes its own way. In a slowed-down state we are often able to observe our own thoughts. After a while, we can interrupt a thought process, track it back to the beginning, and gain insight into its cause and driving force. Invariably, we will discover the rudimentary elements of our thoughts are attraction or avoidance, just like that little amoeba, but much more complicated.

How do we know when the self is identified with the "wanting mind"? First, the fact that the mind is engaged in discursive thought is an almost certain giveaway of the presence of self-involvement, except in those rare in-stances where contemplation is on the higher, spiritual realms. If this self-involvement is not clear to us at first, the language and images used in our thinking will confirm it. Look for the "I/me" language or image that is present in the thought either as subject or as object. Meditators soon realize that an astonishing amount of time is spent returning to endlessly cycling cravings.

The natural biological functions that operate from a balanced center are usually expressed and fulfilled in a short period. The need to eat or drink something is gratified relatively soon. The need to breathe is almost instantly met. The requirements we attend to quickly do not linger. The aspirations that extend outward, however, dwelling and constantly reappearing in our thoughts, are much more likely to be a product of "wanting mind" and self-involvement.

One of the advantages of regularly scheduled meditation, and certainly of retreat, is that we have the opportunity to observe our mental process in action over and over and over again. At first, we are so accustomed to our own incessant inner conversations, we do not realize the source or even the content of much of our thought. When we begin to pay attention, we detect patterns in what appeared to be scattered thoughts. We begin to see that many of the thoughts are nothing more than old rags wrapped around a basic ambition that finds expression through fantasies. These fantasies seem quite real while they last.

Once completed, our thought-rags are discarded but a new fantasy soon arises, wrapped in different rags. This thought may have a fresh appearance, but the vagabond inside is the same old desire-body. When we are able to pay close attention, the thought disappears. We become quiet for a minute, but very soon a new fragment jumps into our consciousness. We may finish with that, and possibly the original thought-rag reappears for act two, act three, and so forth. These are familiar rags that we assumed were already in the garbage heap. On and on we continue to take voyages through the dumping grounds. After a period of this kind of exploration, we often experience the shock of recognition of the amount of time we spend in our mental garbage heap. New images pop up constantly, sometimes wrapped in gorgeous finery— but still, in the end, the vagabond inside will be revealed as aspiration, lust, greed, gluttony, or ambition.

Sounds depressing, doesn't it? When we are blithely moving along in our everyday mind, the same process takes place, but we do not notice it. It is happening this very moment. If you put this book down for a minute or two, close your eyes, and try to be perfectly quiet— behold, here comes a thought. Try to grasp one thought as it races past. Hold it for a second. What is really going on here? Can you find an "I want," or "I wish," or "If only I" hidden somewhere in this thought? Look closely: the identification is usually quite subtle. Try another thought. What do you get out of this one? Can you detect the desire hidden in it? If you look closely, you will probably find it.

We soon establish that desire is almost always present. Even when we try to sit quietly, we want to be quiet. This too is a desire because we would like all the busy thoughts to go away. If we are seeking tranquillity, then incessant thoughts are a real nuisance. Our longing for silence may make us anxious, frustrated, or depressed. But trying to get rid of our longing is also a desire. We must find a way out of this trap, to release ourselves without becoming attached to the release. This is a tricky proposition.

In Buddhism the "wanting mind" is one of the five major hindrances encountered by a meditator. The first skill we need to develop is to learn how to refrain from instinctively pushing this or other unpleasant mind states away. We need not try to avoid them, nor even wish they would go away. The wanting mind and other negative mind states are simply what they are and we must learn to be comfortable with them.

Another method is to reflect on our urges just long enough to give them a name. We could use a general label, such as "desire"; or we could use something more specific, such as "wanting to be rich" or "wishing I were famous." After a while, we will begin to spot thematic repetitions. Then we can make a mental note, "wanting to be rich, AGAIN!" or "wishing I were famous, ONE MORE TIME!" We observe the repetition not as a self-judgment, but in a wry, pragmatic, somewhat amused manner.

Desire-generated thoughts run unimpeded when they are not observed. When we become skilled in this kind of recognition and the patterns grow familiar, we begin to catch the thoughts somewhere in the middle, or even soon after they begin. Without any judgment or attempt to drive the thoughts out, our observation will have an inhibiting effect. Once we pay attention to our thought process, it slowly begins to behave itself.

Some persistent thought modalities drag us along kicking and screaming; they have their own energy source and will. This is particularly true of desires deeply embedded in our psyches. Lust is a common demon often difficult to subdue. Personal power is another rascal constantly peeking at us from our mind-mirrors. Some traditional practices recommend using visualization to defeat desire when it seems to be intractable. A common method of dealing with lust, for example, is to imagine the sexual object covered with disgusting sores, leprosy, skin falling off—nothing but skeleton, muscle, and feces. It does not take long to quell lust with this kind of imagery. This may sound melodramatic to someone unfamiliar with meditation, but after sitting for long hours or days obsessed with the same idea, we are often willing to take extreme measures.

Unbounded desire is an implacable enemy with a deviousness that can never be underestimated. We can employ visualization, mantra, and restraint to master it. However, we must always remember that although an enemy, aspiration cannot be defeated through opposition but only through "psychological" warfare. The best defense is to understand the enemy, know how it works, where it comes from, how we feel when it is near, what it uses for camouflage, what attracts it, when it flees? All of this we can learn in quiet, careful meditation practice, which is amplified in a retreat setting.

Desire is always waiting in the wings and when given the slightest nod, it leaps to center stage. The most experienced meditators still have to deal with this devilish character. We come to understand that the nature of our sensory apparatus is to grasp and cling to incoming stimuli. All our sensory input is based on an intrinsic desire modality.

The master learns how to see, hear, touch, taste, and smell the essence of life without adding the slightest nuance of "I/me." The stimuli come and go without associations, memories, comparisons; the master has no feeling of attraction and no sense of avoidance, no measuring, analyzing, or evaluating. Everything that arises in a moment is just exactly what it is for that moment, nothing more, nothing less. This is the state of choiceless awareness—awareness without desire.

Working with desire rests on learning how to work with the senses. Everything that comes into the mind has the potential to arouse craving. The Buddhists add an additional avenue of sensory input to the five basic senses of seeing, hearing, smelling, tasting, and touching. The mind itself somehow has a self-stimulating faculty. Without any external input, through some unknown mechanism, the mind wanders over immense internal fields and wastelands. The physiology of this process is connected with a sixth sense in Buddhist psychology, not in the way the sixth sense is commonly used in the West as a level of intuition, but as another sensory organ. Just as we must learn how to relate to the sensory input from the five external senses, so too we must learn to recognize the impulses of the mind, which themselves may ignite and stimulate our desires.

When we become acutely sensitized on an extended retreat, we are often able to trace a thought back to the initial stimulation that aroused it. After a while, we are able to notice desire responses almost immediately. This observation inhibits the "wanting mind" and it dies as quickly as it was born. Without this awareness, the aspiration will follow its usual course, which often involves the generation of thoughts or obsessions related to it. The more we are able to observe desire arising and quickly fading away, the more our true appreciation of its nature will deepen. This awareness is a key element in the process of liberation.

Simply said, desire is our nemesis only when we are identified with it, when an "I/me" element drives it beyond its organic function; it runs rampant only when it operates unobserved. Thus the process of freeing our minds from unbounded longings is based on quiet and continuous internal observation. This alone heightens awareness, and as the new awareness adds strength to our power of observation, we ultimately gain a true release from enslavement to our desires.

# AVERSION

The opposite face of desire is aversion. Wherever we find desire, there is always some aversion; wherever we notice aversion, there is always some desire. For example, if we want something, the aversion side is to avoid disappointment; conversely, if we are repelled by something, the desire aspect is that we wish to get away from it.

From a purely academic perspective, the only real difference between desire and aversion is the focus of our attention. If most of our attention is directed toward wanting something, such as money, we call it desire for wealth rather than aversion to poverty. If we are trying to push away pain, we call it aversion to pain rather than desire for painlessness.

The quality of the desire experience, however, differs significantly from the aversion experience. The experience of desire increases hopes, expectations, and aspirations that lead to anxiety, frustration, and a sense of futility if they are not satisfied. At its extreme, desire expresses itself as greed, gluttony, and lust. On the other side, the quality of aversion increases the sense of rejection, avoidance, and the flight mechanism that leads to feelings of being trapped, exasperation, and anger. At its extreme, aversion expresses itself as hostility, fear, paranoia, and hatred.

UNPLEASANT MIND STATES

While on retreat, these experiences are greatly magnified. We may find ourselves in a rage one minute and deep in universal love the next. In the beginning stages of meditation this can be confusing, and we may feel tossed about like a ball. There may also be long periods with no fluctuations, which can be equally confusing: "Where did this lust come from? I'm really not a very nice person! What horrible thoughts! I would not dare tell anyone! Why all this hatred? Am I really like this? If anyone could see into my mind, I would be locked up!"

After a while, watching the patterns repeat, observing the wild swings of emotion, noticing how often thoughts or feelings seem to arise by themselves, we begin to cast a wary eye on our own thought process. The gates of realization open, and through the crack we see a light that indicates a frightening notion: Most of our thoughts are a function of mechanical conditioning and automatic response. This insight works slowly to diminish our tendency to identify with our thoughts.

We in the West tend to be analytical about ourselves. We try to understand how all the pieces fit together, what makes us tick. Meditation and retreat experiences provide a wealth of material for self-analysis and psychological exploration. As a result, a great deal of time and energy is spent in a sea of critical analysis. A large number of meditators attempt a retreat as a therapeutic process. This usually results in a cul-de-sac of self-indulgence and endless introspection.

The Eastern approach is much more intuitive since there is hardly any interest in psychoanalytical implications. The basic principle of the intuitive process is that intellectual analysis is the complete reverse of what we are working toward in meditation. The intellect impedes us from achieving balance and harmony, and it strengthens the grasping or averting nature of the mind. As long as our thought process is turned in on itself, we have no chance of gaining true insight from the intuitive perspective of "emptiness."

The aim is to observe the thoughts but not to identify with them. If we refrain from identifying with our thoughts, we have no basis for self-analysis. They are merely reflections of mind activity. From this vantage point, we are able to observe how thoughts arise and how they gain their momentum.

It is difficult to approach thought as a specimen to be examined, for a thought will not rest passively on the microscope slide. Often, the thought will evaporate just as we are trying to adjust the lens. When we notice this, we begin to gain insight into the energy driving many of our thoughts. Thoughts do not have any energy of their own. If we relinquish our identification with them, we stop feeding them, and they disappear.

When a thought is relatively subtle, it disappears so rapidly we usually miss it; it is often difficult to recall the thought at all. Also, we are less likely to identify with subtle thoughts, as they tend to be more abstract.

We are more identified with conspicuous thoughts, such as anger or hatred. This is where we can really work with the practice and where the greatest insight is born. The meditative technique is not an attempt to understand the anger nor cure it (although this may indeed be the result), but rather to observe it without judgment— simply a cool, somewhat distant, examination of its elements.

The first step is to be able to notice thoughts as they arise in our minds. Most of the time, when we are not observing thoughts, they simply come and go. We often do not realize we have been fuming for some time. Many meditation practices strengthen our inner observer. Even though we constantly slip away in our minds while meditating, losing ourselves for periods of time, we inevitably come back to the observer and thereby increase our skill in distinguishing thoughts as they occur.

Once we know we are in an angry state of mind, the next stage of observation begins. This is a fascinating level of meditation. The mind is still identified with the anger, yet the observer has just enough strength to remain aware for short intervals. At this stage, we can examine more carefully the rationalizing, justifying, and self-righteous indignation of our angry mind. We can discern how this mechanism builds worlds of hatred, scenes of destruction, fantasies of revenge.

Sometimes the observer blinks and we slip into a long period of non-awareness. The mind goes on a rampage—we live entirely in the world of anger we have created. We become completely oblivious to everything around us. This may last brief moments or long minutes; it can last an entire meditation period of an hour. In some retreats, an obsessive mind state can be the predominant feature for many days. We believe that it will never be resolved; we will carry it with us forever. Then, months or years later, we glance through a journal we kept during that retreat, and we vaguely remember how we felt at that time about someone who is now our spouse or best friend.

This process of simply watching our anger or any other emotion builds its own momentum. As we understand more what our rampant emotions require as a source of fuel, we learn how to starve those that are detrimental to our well-being. When we gain insight into the initial cause of our anger, for example, we are more able to intercept it before it catches us. We realize how anger tightens the mind and body, we learn to recognize cues that will awaken us when we are asleep. The more this insight develops, the more we realize we do not have to be overwhelmed by anger; it can come and go in a flash.

It is significant to realize that anger will arise as a natural response. If we place a negative value on anger, if we judge it, then we have added to our burden. A negative judgment about something means we have an aversion toward it, and this will fuel the emotion itself. We will be unhappy with ourselves for being angry and will try to discover how to avoid it. But, if we recognize it as a normal response in certain situations, then anger simply is what it is. Our work is not to eliminate it, but to develop the skills to observe its nature—we neither identify with anger nor try to push it away. If we do this, the anger comes and goes in its own time, but our emotional attachment is minimized.

This does not mean that we neutralize our emotions, but that we do not confuse appropriate emotions with tangential issues. Anger and even hatred may begin as a healthy aversion to issues such as fascism, rape, murder, or child abuse. In fact, anger may save lives when an event necessitates violent response. But when we have distance from an event and the emotion overflows into our thoughts causing us to feel bile rising and turning our stomachs queasy, we have become attached and identified—there is no opportunity to develop awareness under these circumstances.

Management of aversion is the crucial issue. If a normal response of strong aversion degenerates into mindless behavior, prejudice, tightness, and obsessive thought, then the aversion is not being treated with awareness. If we observe an aversion as it arises, gain some understanding of our reaction during the process, and then watch the

UNPLEASANT MIND STATES

aversion fade away, we gain wisdom and spiritual insight.

A spiritual aspirant encounters aversion frequently, often in the form of simple dislikes or preferences. They may seem important, but upon closer inspection they are seen to be insignificant in comparison with the suffering in the world. As we gain experience, we become aware that some periods are more filled with aversion than others and that at these times we have a general tightness of being, which affects our perception.

This can lead to the deep understanding that we affect our surroundings by our physical presence. The constriction caused by our aversions works two ways: The incoming stimuli are more likely to arouse dislike because of the negative filters wrapped around our sensory apparatus, and our tenseness radiates negative "energy" that causes every being around us to react. This is a self-perpetuating situation. We are neither its cause nor its victim. We are part of a system, like the spoke on a wheel; we support the wheel as much as we are caught in it. Nonetheless, we *do* have a way to extricate ourselves from this wheel.

We have the power to reduce or eliminate our constriction through quiet observation. When we do so, the softening affects not only our state of mind, but also our environment. This is a great secret of the enlightenment process. Things are what they are, but the world around us and the entire universe reverberates with every new insight and moment of clarity.

This does not happen through analysis but springs forth as an understanding, a powerful intuition. It comes as a rush of awareness, a *satori* experience that breaks upon new vistas, causing a major paradigm shift, forever changing how we approach life. And it is accomplished simply by observing our thoughts, using the techniques of concentration and effort, and working with the raw materials provided by desire and aversion.

In the early stages of spiritual development, we can use various practices to deal with the tight, avoiding mind. Visualizations can reprogram images into greater acceptance and loving kindness. Mantras work well; the power of the sound penetrates our consciousness. Movement is also an excellent practice, as the physical demands will pull the mind out of self-involvement. In the long run, however, it is helpful to gain clear perspective on the true nature of the aversion and not simply to overwhelm it with powerful practices.

One of the most common aversions that arises in many spiritual practices and especially in the context of retreats is pain. Because this is such a problem for so many people, it warrants a separate evaluation.

# PAIN

Pain is experienced at the physical, emotional, and psychological levels. Although the focus in this chapter is on physical pain, the methods of dealing with it are generally applicable to the emotional and psychological experiences as well.

In almost every retreat setting, when the time comes for questions from participants, somebody will ask a question about pain. Everybody in the room is usually sympathetic, because we all experience physical discomfort at one point or another during our sitting. As we are highly sensitized in the retreat process, our distress is typically more acute than our normal daily experiences.

The pain is often centered somewhere in the legs, usually at a joint. Many people also experience back, shoulder, and neck cramps, but pain can materialize anywhere. People experience aches in their cheeks, foreheads, eyelids, ears, toes, scalp, and internal organs; it is amazing what new vistas are opened up when we sit quietly, doing nothing.

Zen teacher Philip Kapleau discusses this issue in answer to the following question: "After a few minutes of sitting, I found a sharp pain coming up into the left side of my head. This happened every time a new round of sitting started."

His answer:

### PAIN

*In the beginning sensitive persons often have twinges of pain in different parts of their body, owing to pre-existing tensions in those areas and the strain of turning one's energies inward instead of dispersing them outwardly. It is also a strain at first for body and mind to function as a unity in* zazen. *If this discomfort is accompanied by feelings of apprehension, the pain and tension increase. When you understand the reasons for the increased tension and resultant pain, and are aware that they are only temporary, the fear will evaporate. Naturally the pain will also disappear and be replaced with a sense of buoyancy and well-being.*[7]

In our practice, we come to understand that pain appears naturally throughout daily activity. It comes and goes, sometimes lasting only moments, at other times for extended periods. In many instances, some level of physical discomfort is a regular companion of our wakeful hours.

The normal experience of pain is intensified if we are in a contracted mind state, such as fear, anxiety, disquiet, or panic, including any mind state that would fall under the general category of aversion. If we are unhappy with what is happening at any particular moment, the suffering is usually increased. If we are holding anger and frustration within, the sensation of physical harm increases. This becomes a serious matter when the distress itself is the source of the aversion. Then the intensity compounds rapidly. The pain and the aversion feed on each other until we are compelled to respond.

Kapleau discusses another aspect:

*Also remember that your discomfort can be a trick of the ego to derail your practice. Since the ego does not wish to lose its cozy dominance, it throws up all sorts of barriers to retain control, the most common of which is pain, for it knows that persistent* zazen *will terminate its rule. If you recognize that the pain is only a device of the ego to get you to quit, you can turn the tables on this wily*

UNPLEASANT MIND STATES

*phantom by refusing to give in. Pain is a challenge that sooner or later must be met, and the way to banish it is to become fully one with it.*[8]

This is an important idea in spiritual practice. We have an aspect within us that is accustomed to being in control; this part expresses likes and dislikes and elicits familiar responses. We sometimes call it the ego. In this instance, the idea of "ego" represents the sense a person has of "I/me" rather than the way the word *ego* is used in modern psychology, which is related to the personality. Thus, when teachers discuss the necessity of dissolving or annihilating the ego, they are referring to the identity we have with an "I" or "me" of substance.

The ego spins in its own universe. It identifies with a complex set of preferences: "I know myself because I like this and I do not like that." The ego is so identified with preferences that a strong challenge to these beliefs will often prove traumatic.

Except for the normal friction of the aging process, once the ego has found its spin, it will resist any adjustment. When this inner spin is disturbed, as occurs in various stages of meditation, the ego's sense of itself falls into jeopardy, and we begin to wobble—our nicely balanced spinning top has been bumped. The ego's response to this wobble is immediate, and the weapons in its arsenal are far-reaching. The experienced and committed aspirant will sooner or later come to realize that the ego is fighting for its existence. It will go to any extreme to survive.

For example, when we sit quietly our habitual desires and aversions will begin to express themselves in our thoughts. If we are following a conscientious discipline and are successful in the process of reconditioning our internal responses, we will break the pattern that is familiar to the ego, and a new sensation will occur in the body. This is the beginning stage of the higher states of awareness, but its newness disturbs the spinning ego, which does not like change. Thus we will have a reaction.

We may suddenly notice a fluttering in the chest. Soon it becomes a sharp ache, and in the twinkling of an eye we think we are having a heart attack. The mind twists in fear until we settle down and realize that the ache is probably nothing more than a minor complaint. But this experience may cause us to think this is a good time to visit the doctor just to be sure.

Once again we are sitting quietly and suddenly we remember an incident that happened twenty-five years ago. Within minutes we are enjoying a fantasy or we are filled with a rage. Then we realize we are merely sitting, watching our breath. In another moment, the spasm in the left knee becomes intense. "I'll never make it through without moving." "I wonder if I have cancer, God forbid." "My knee is getting ruined." "This isn't worth a lifetime limp." "What a waste of time; nothing is different now from when I started." "Oh, the knee really hurts; if only it would stop!"

On and on the internal dialogue goes—filled with doubts, fears, confusion, and aversion. The ego pushes and prods, looking for vulnerable responses, imploring us to stop, tricking us, doing anything to maintain the same old spin. If I lose control, I believe that "I won't know who I am anymore." Our sense of identity comes from familiar responses to likes and dislikes. This is who we think we are. If we do not react in a familiar way, then we have nothing to relate to as "me."

The spiritual path always has an aspect of death and rebirth. The death of the "I/me" and the birth into a new entity is the archetypal process of spiritual discovery.

### UNPLEASANT MIND STATES

This process almost always involves anguish, often physical pain, and usually emotional or psychological grief as well. In many primitive societies, the initiation rites into the higher mysteries involve surrender to an ordeal, sometimes actual torture and mutilation. Withstanding and overcoming this affliction is an essential part of the path.

Mircea Eliade points out:

> *We find that individual mystical callings . . . follow . . . the scenario: sufferings, tortures, death, and resurrection. And this leads us to conclude that the mystery of spiritual regeneration involves an archetypal process that is enacted on different levels and in numerous contexts whenever a man must transcend one mode of being to arrive at another, higher one, or, more precisely, whenever there is a question of spiritual transmutation.*[9]

Pain is an intrinsic element in the process of enlightenment. Yet, a healthy person does not like suffering and certainly does not want to invite it in. We saw earlier that gaining insight into the causes of pain relieves a large amount of it, and this opens a new level of well-being. However, a continuous feeling of well-being may retard our spiritual growth. This contradiction was articulated by G. I. Gurdjieff:

> *A man will renounce any pleasures you like but he will not give up his suffering. Man is made in such a way that he is never so much attached to anything as he is to his suffering. And it is necessary to be free from suffering. No one who is not free from suffering, who has not sacrificed his suffering, can work [on himself]. . . . Nothing can be attained without suffering but at the same time one must begin by sacrificing suffering.*[10]

We cannot attain anything without some degree of suffering, yet if we are not free from suffering we cannot work on ourselves. How can we reconcile these contrary views? There are two basic approaches to this difficult issue and they both address the same point, which is: Who is suffering?

In the Buddhist approach, the pain we experience becomes the object of the meditation. Many Buddhist teachers are uninterested in our meditation experiences except for pain. What is its quality? Where is it precisely located? What are its exact sensations? Does it seem to increase or decrease when our full attention is put on it? When does it begin and when does it disappear? What do we do when the pain is overwhelming?

This analytical approach to the phenomenon of pain leads to great insight into its nature. Often when we begin to focus on it, two paths open: We realize how much we have been trying to avoid it, and we discover how difficult pain is to pin down and identify. In other words, we spend an enormous amount of energy trying to avoid something we never really get to know. Pain is something so repugnant to us, we begin to run the moment we feel its outer edges. As soon as we have a hint of discomfort, our very act of running creates the illusion of substance out of shadow.

There are innumerable "breakthrough" stories where someone was sitting in excruciating misery, and then, all of a sudden, it disappeared. That moment is filled with blessed joy, partially because of the release from the suffering, more significantly because of the recognition that most of the suffering was a phantom induced by the mind itself.

At that stage, we begin to recognize the usefulness of pain, how it helps us shatter the image of self, and we enter a new relationship with our essential nature. Here

UNPLEASANT MIND STATES

the question of "Who is suffering?" is pertinent. A large amount of suffering vanishes with the release of self-identity.

It follows that suffering can be viewed as an important motivator in the enlightenment process. It can be appreciated as our helpmate to push us to the limits necessary to break the grip of a tenacious ego. Most teachers acknowledge the extraordinary difficulty aspirants experience in shedding self-identity. Thus, pain is a helpful psychic instrument that can reveal our true nature, and it can be the single most powerful resource to break the tenacious grip of self-identity.

Another approach is brought through Hasidic wisdom teachings:

> My master revealed to me that when a person has pain, whether physical or spiritual, he should meditate that even in this pain, God can be found. He [God] is only concealed in a garment in the pain. When a person realizes this, then he can remove the garment. The pain and all evil decrees can then be nullified.[11]

The pain is not "mine" but a garment in which the divine may be discovered. This too probes the question, "Who is suffering?" Letting go helps us realize we are not what we thought we were.

The comprehension of all forms of distress is of enormous value in the process of spiritual unfolding. However, we must always keep in mind that the person in pain is really suffering. To her or him, it is not an illusion. When we are despondent, or racked with intense pain, it is impossible to be objective. Thus, the abstractions of the true nature of suffering are irrelevant in many situations.

When trying to help someone, we are obliged to work within that person's reality and frame of reference. Our heightened awareness and appreciation that God is "in the pain" should not prevent us from attempting everything possible to help this person. All teachers recommend working with compassion and loving kindness in this situation. Indeed, wisdom teachings in both Buddhist and Christian traditions suggest that the act of compassion and loving kindness is a direct path of enlightenment—even though in Buddhism the basis of the compassion is coming out of and being applied to an illusion. More grist for the mill in the universe of spiritual paradox.

Pain, therefore, not only provides the impetus for us to break through our self-limitations, but it can also arouse empathy in those around us and be the source of compassion that helps them break through their own constrictions.

The gap between theory and practice is described by an older Zen student whose account appears in *The Three Pillars of Zen*:

> *When the sesshin [a Zen-oriented retreat] began . . . it turned out to be something I had never imagined. It was, as a matter of fact, torture. It so happens that several of the joints of my legs are permanently stiff from two automobile accidents. This, together with the fact that I was almost sixty at the time, made sitting with my legs crossed in the lotus posture excruciating. (Still, thinking about it afterward, I know that whatever I gained came to me through this pain.) I experienced the worst in my legs at dawn of the second day. Feeling that death itself could not be worse, I told myself: "All this pain comes from zazen, and you can escape it if you wish. But if you were dying and in agony, you would be unable to escape the suffering, so bear this pain in the same spirit and die if need be!" I fought this torment with every ounce of strength.*[12]

This narrative is archetypal. An inexperienced meditator has no notion of what to expect on a retreat. Even well-exercised, supple legs have problems adjusting, but sitting in a full lotus position with injured joints invites a serious encounter with the pain demon. Yet, upon reflection, this meditator understood that suffering was a major vehicle for what he accomplished during the practice. Then, despite the all-consuming quality of the pain, he was able to sustain his effort through sheer determination. His willingness to die is a pivotal point for it breaks all the arguments of self-survival the ego tends to use.

He continued:

> Gradually I felt the pain in my legs less and less as the sesshin progressed, and my mind began to expand until, imperceptibly, it reached a sublime state . . . I felt as though I were in paradise. . . . Involuntarily I began to cry softly, then the tears streamed down my cheeks. . . . After the sesshin I mentioned this crying episode to the roshi. He told me that while I hadn't yet reached the point of kenshō [an enlightenment experience, sometimes called satori], nevertheless I had attained a significant degree of ego attrition.[13]

This was the first retreat experience for this meditator. From pain to paradise in a week's time. He continued in his practice, determined to attain *kenshō*. After eight years of practice and many retreats, he attained a level in a *sesshin* that alerted the roshi to recommend that he sit all night on the last night of the retreat.

> As the evening wore on, the pain in my legs became so grueling that even changing from full- to half-lotus didn't lessen it. My only way of overcoming it was to pour all my energy into single-minded concentration on MU [a classic kōan]. Even with the fiercest concentration to the point of panting "MU! MU! MU!" there was nothing I could do to free myself of the excruciating pain except to shift my posture a little. . . . Abruptly the pains disappear, there is only MU! Each and every thing is MU. "Oh, it's this!" I exclaimed, reeling in astonishment, my mind a total emptiness. . . .

PAIN

*All is freshness and purity itself. Every single object is dancing vividly, inviting me to look. Every single thing occupies its natural place and breathes quietly. . . . They are indescribably beautiful!*[14]

No matter how much we theorize, no matter how many accounts like this we read, we cannot fathom what happens except through direct experience. Our logical mind asks, "How could somebody put himself in painful situations like this, year after year?" We see that even eight years following his initial experience, he was still having to deal with excruciating distress. This confounds our minds and all our theories of the pleasure principle and avoidance of pain.

Psychological theory often breaks down in the face of spiritual endeavor. We have a tendency to try to understand the spiritual domain scientifically. However, the motivation and yearning to be at one with the center of creation, for example, is beyond understanding. The relationship between thought, visualization, or speech as power resources to invoke the manifestation of physical reality is beyond the ken of science. Inviting pain as a friend is something that normative psychology would consider perverted.

The most advanced spiritual beings transcend all human concepts of torment and physical limits. A famous story of Jewish martyrdom concerns Rabbi Akiva, who lived almost two thousand years ago. He was found guilty by the Romans of teaching Torah publicly, a crime punishable by death. The method of capital punishment used on Rabbi Akiva was to strip the flesh from his body, little by little, using sharp iron combs.

*As he lay in unspeakable agony, he suddenly noticed the first streaks of dawn breaking over the eastern hills. It was the hour*

UNPLEASANT MIND STATES

*when the Law requires each Jew to pronounce the* Shema *[the central Jewish prayer, required morning and evening]. Oblivious to his surroundings, Akiva intoned in a loud, steady voice, the forbidden words of his faith, "Hear, O Israel, the Lord is our God, the Lord is One. And thou shalt love the Lord thy God with all thine heart, and with all thy soul, and with all thy might."*[15]

*Rufus, the Roman general, who superintended the horrible execution, cried out, "Are you a wizard or are you utterly insensible to pain?"*

*"I am neither," replied the martyr, "but all my life I have been waiting for the moment when I might truly fulfill this commandment. I have always loved the Lord with all my might, and with all my heart; now I know that I love him with all my life." And, repeating the verse again, he died as he reached the words, "The Lord is One."*[16]

Accounts in all traditions depict superhuman capacity to endure agony. Scientific evidence suggests that beyond a limit, pain can actually kill. Still, the limit is variable dependent upon our level of awareness, our ability to soften the internal resistance, to allow the distress as much room as it demands without pushing it away.

As long as a meditator approaches pain as an enemy, the battle lines will be set, and the skirmishes will end in defeat. When we do not draw battle lines, our discomfort is much more manageable. Adversity will often arise uninvited, but our non-resistance facilitates its departure because nothing is holding on to it and nothing is pushing it away.

This is not easy to learn, but skillfulness comes with practice and perseverance. Our ability to work with suffering is aided by the recognition that everything in the universe is constantly changing, thus we may experience unbearable pain one moment and be in paradise the next. This knowledge, in its most subtle forms, brings us to the realization that just as it is not "my" pain, then "I" do not have to do anything. That is, as long as we identify with suffering, then we believe we must do something to get rid of it; when pain is just pain and it does not belong to me, then it will come and go on its own.

Obviously, this is not referring to pain that is part of our survival mechanism. The fire that burns, the sharp edge that cuts—there are important responses that keep us from hurting ourselves even more. Upon examination, however, even this discomfort is our friend. One of the worst illnesses children can have is the inability to feel pain. Such people suffer traumatic body damage without recognizing it. They usually do not live full lifespans because they lack warning mechanisms.

Affliction of any kind remains baffling for the beginner in meditation. We have spent our lives trying to avoid uncomfortable situations. Despite all the teachings, the reality of experience continues to be the best teacher, well beyond all words and theory. After a while, pain becomes a fact of life. We learn to note it for what it is, and then move on; it no longer dominates us and we certainly do not dominate it. Discomfort is one of many familiar cues that aid us in our meditation, helping us to recognize our mind states. We learn to use pain as a built-in bio-feedback mechanism, noticing how it is affected by our breathing, concentration, relaxation, visualization, mantras, and especially by the soft or hard quality of our minds. This is why pain is ultimately a great friend and teacher. It is a perfect, moment-to-moment reflection of our mind state, and it raises our level of consciousness through its incessant demands.

# FEAR

A major aversion that meditators experience—less common but much more insidious than pain—is fear. Pain often leads to fear, but many levels of apprehension have limited, if any, association with pain. Even great pleasure can make us afraid that if we enjoy ourselves too much, we will pay with suffering.

Fear is part of our basic survival mechanism. Appropriate fear falls into two categories, one of which is shared by all forms of life. When something threatens living beings, the "fight or flight" response is invoked. Its main feature is immediacy, because the link between the threat and the response is clear. If we are walking in the woods and a bear rears up in front of us, the rush of terror that flushes through us is not something we have to think about.

The other category of appropriate fear is exclusively human. It is the anxiety generated by imagination, fed by the experience of life. We have all had the experience of falling down, but few of us have fallen off a building or seen somebody else suffer such an accident. Yet, we can extrapolate from our own experience of falling and imagine what it would feel like to drop from a great height. This induces a level of trepidation that keeps us from jumping off tall buildings. Appropriate fear, like this, is one kind of common sense.

A toddler or young child does not have much of this common sense respect because she or he has not had enough experience to fuel the imagination. A large part of parenting is the protection of the fearless child and the transmission of experience to instill suitable alarms. Many theories of child psychology advise us how best to train a child, but they all involve some kind of experience that adds dimension to the child's imagination.

We need more than direct experience. Conversation, rumor, and storytelling also feed our fantasy. Most of the concerns we have, like smashing our fingers in a car door, are not things we have ever directly experienced, but our imaginations are quite graphic on the subject. Just thinking about it can often bring queasiness to our stomachs and perhaps a feeling of light-headedness. We may not be able to identify exactly why, but we are afraid of opening a gorilla's cage and walking in, even though the gorilla appears to be completely harmless, sitting there quietly munching a banana.

There are times, however, when our imagination exceeds its appropriate boundaries. This often happens when our minds are confused because of stress, illness, or drugs, but it can happen at any time in a normal escalation of emotion. Then our imaginative faculty conjures up an entirely new personal reality in which our normal common sense does not function because the fear response has become distorted. This reality may cause us to feel completely vulnerable in an evil world and to withdraw into a corner of imagined protection. Conversely, we may become absolutely fearless in this confused reality. This can become truly dangerous if we believe, for example, it is possible for humans to fly from buildings or drive safely at one hundred miles an hour. Under this illusion many people have hurt or killed themselves—or others—without the slightest hesitation. Their fear response was not operating properly.

Our marvelous imaginative ability, which gives us a distinct survival advantage over other forms of life, can cause us enormous grief. It often generates dread well beyond the needs of survival, and it perverts our fears into inappropriate patterns. This amplification of apprehension applies not only to worry of physical harm, but extends to a wide range of psychological anxieties having to do with relationship or self-image.

When we begin to meditate, we discover how much our lives are dominated by worry. While a small percentage of this is appropriate, most is clearly out of proportion. Apprehension so thoroughly permeates our lives that we often fail to recognize the true source of our motivation. When we are able to sit quietly on retreat, our ability to trace our mental process improves and we understand more clearly the associations that empower our thoughts and beliefs. An examination of these associations often reveals anxiety at the core.

As our experience develops, we gain insight into the nature of fear. In the beginning, however, many hours of meditation may be filled with strong misgivings, anxieties, and even paranoia. On an intensive retreat, an altered mind state may magnify our anxiety so completely out of proportion that our will may be crushed. Occasionally, this experience is powerful enough to cause the early termination of a retreat.

The discussion that follows applies to inappropriate fear, which is often characterized by two major elements: misinformation and/or delay. Imagination based on unreliable information can produce a level of apprehension not relevant to the situation. The shorter the delay-time between something that causes uneasiness and the response, the more likely our reaction will be appropriate; the longer the gap, the more time the imagination has to develop and the more likely our response will be inappropriate. This is not a hard and fast rule, but a general principle.

When sitting on retreat, the knowledge of these two factors is helpful in observing and distinguishing our mind state. If we are not able to recognize the anxiety, it will overwhelm us, and, as with pain and other strong aversions, we will find it more difficult to be objective. Pain draws our attention in a relatively focused way while fear is more amorphous. Accordingly, if we ask ourselves "Am I in immediate danger?" or "How well do I understand all the factors here?" we are often able to gain enough distance to be objective about it.

Our identification with apprehension, as with any other self-identification, brings about the illusion of separateness. This hardens the boundary between us and everything outside ourselves. If that sense of boundary did not exist, there would be nothing to fear.

The phrase "nothing to fear" is a play on words. At first we understand it to mean that we need not be afraid of anything outside ourselves, but then we realize that if there is no-thing, i.e., no self-identity, no "I/me," then there is no-thing, no "I/me" to be afraid.

Many teachers discuss this issue in terms of dissolving the ego. Ramana Maharshi said:

> *What is fear? It is only a thought. If there is anything beside the [One] there is reason to fear. Who sees things separate from the [One]? First the ego arises and sees objects as external. If the ego does not rise, the [One] alone exists and there is nothing external.*[17]

The practical advice given by Ramana Maharshi is to recognize that any sense of the external implies a "seer" within. If we focus all our attention on this seer, in other words, asking the question "Who is afraid?" we will realize that there is no real separation, and then all doubt and apprehension will vanish. Moreover, he says, "Not only fear, but all other thoughts centered around the ego will disappear along with it."

An integral relationship exists between insecurity and fear. Krishnamurti speaks forcefully on this issue:

> There is fear as long as you want to be secure—secure in your marriage, secure in your job, in your position, in your responsibility, secure in your ideas, in your beliefs, secure in your relationship to the world or in your relationship to God. The moment the mind seeks security or gratification in any form, at any level, there is bound to be fear. . . .[18]

Grasping for security in an ever-changing world assures a continuous state of anxiety. Alan Watts wrote a book called *The Wisdom of Insecurity* which speaks to this issue, showing that the only way we can free ourselves from anxiety is to accept insecurity as an essential truth.

The acceptance of constant insecurity is a heroic act. The hero is always stepping into the unknown—risking death—to gain greater insight. If we accept a constant state of insecurity as our truth, fear is perpetually banished.

Another approach is to devote ourselves to God. William James describes the concept of "friendliness" with God:

> In the Christian consciousness this sense of the enveloping friendliness becomes most personal and definite. "The compensation," writes a German author, "for the loss of that sense of personal independence which man so unwillingly gives up, is the disappearance of all fear from one's life, the quite indescribable and inexplicable feeling of an inner security, which one can only

*experience, but which, once it has been experienced, one can never forget."*[19]

This is another reflection of breaking down the barriers of ego and joining with the divine. A scriptural source of this idea was suggested by the nineteenth-century Hasidic master Mordecai Joseph Leiner of Izbica. He examines the passage in Exodus where the Hebrew midwives refuse to follow Pharaoh's edict to kill all newborn male children. The verse says, "And it came to pass, because the midwives feared God, that He made them houses."[20] What does it mean that "He made them houses"?

Reb Mordecai suggests:

> *When a man is afraid of other human beings his soul lacks serenity, since fear is a direct contradiction to serenity of mind. But serenity is found where there is the fear of God, blessed be He. This is why it says: "and He made them houses." A house denotes serenity of mind. Since they had this serenity, the fruit of their fear of God, Pharaoh's decree had no terrors for them.*[21]

This concept of fearing God is a common theme in Western religious tradition. It is often misunderstood to imply quavering timidity or pious foreboding; God is envisioned as a glowering force ready to crush any slight infraction of the law. Mystics in the Western tradition, however, invariably express it as the dread of isolation rather than punishment. Actual punishment, in its way, is a sign of God's love, just as a parent tries to teach a child a lesson. What could be worse than a complete withdrawal and abandonment? Hence, the fear of God means the concern of being separate, locked into the alienated ego.

Rabbi Louis Jacobs, who is one of the most prolific contemporary authors on Hasidism, points out:

> *The accusation that religion is based on fear is countered by noting that, in fact, the fear of God is such that it frees man from all*

*other fears. It produces the serenity and peace of mind that enables man to face all obstacles calmly and courageously just as the midwives who feared God were indifferent to Pharaoh's orders that they should kill the Hebrew infants.*[22]

When we understand that Pharaoh in Judaism represents the power of Evil Incarnate, we gain a broader appreciation of the depth of surrender we would have to make to fend off this force.

An exceptional approach to fear was expressed by the Baal Shem Tov, the founder of the Hasidic movement. He taught that every arising thought has a divine spark, however deeply hidden. Thus, for the Baal Shem Tov, the aim is not to transform our fears, or even to eliminate them, but to acknowledge that fear has a higher source. This is a highly esoteric idea of multileveled universes in which every thought has the possibility of becoming attached to God.

*If it involves desire and lust, it has fallen from the Universe of Love; if it is a debilitating phobia, it is from the Universe of Fear; and if it involves pride, it is from the Universe of Beauty. The same is true of all other such thoughts, since [the attributes paralleling] all seven days of creation have fallen. When you bind these thoughts to God through love and fear of the Creator, you then return them to their Root.*[23]

Notice that the Baal Shem Tov does not rate the Universe of Fear lower than that of Love or Beauty. They are all root aspects of creation, and as such are divine. Thus we need to embrace our fear rather than avoid it. We need to put on new glasses in order to perceive its divine sparks. No matter what the cause or manifestation, as long as we understand that its source is in the Universe of Fear, the divine realm, we will gain a new perspective.

One principle underlies all these methods—do not

identify with the fear. It is not "my fear," or that "I am afraid"; it should instead be characterized as "here is fear" or "fear is rising." Once we gain detachment, our emotional experiences become a tool to help bind us with the Oneness, with God.

One of the main qualities of spiritual liberation is the release from the suffering of inappropriate fear. Although other levels of spiritual accomplishment often resist our efforts, many retreatants have significant success in working with anxiety, apprehension, distrust, and dread. This may be due to the nature of these feelings. They tend to spread rapidly when uncontrolled, but they are relatively manageable with moderate effort. We may not experience this early in a retreat, but after a while fear in all its variations will respond to the spiritual medicine recommended above.

# DEMONIC VISIONS

Strange, bizarre, and often gruesome visual images are not uncommon phenomena during intensive meditations or retreats. Spiritual practices have a powerful effect on our normal state of mind; in a relatively short time we begin to experience altered states of consciousness. Sensory input is filtered differently, mental processing works in an unusual way, and our entire outlook is dramatically modified.

Not only are our waking hours affected, so is our sleep. Often sleep is agitated, with a nervous buzz, and sometimes dreams are wild. Dreaming may begin before we fall asleep. As soon as our eyes close a rapid sequence of images may race through our minds; at times thousands of faces or events flash by in a few seconds. Many people find this bewildering while others think it is downright scary.

When an intensive practice lasts for more than a few days, sleep patterns are usually affected and waking hours are more dreamlike. In the altered state, a new quality of awareness begins to predominate. This is not wakefulness as we know it, nor is it sleep. This mind state has not been studied much, yet it is a common experience for many retreatants. With our different frame of reference, we are more acutely aware of what is happening in the moment;

there seems to be more time to accomplish what we need to do as well as appreciate everything around us. In fact, time seems to expand as our awareness expands.

Just as Einstein discussed the relativity of time in physical terms, esoteric doctrines discuss the relativity of time in psychic terms. Ultimately, time is transcended when we truly integrate with the here and now. Here and now is timeless, infinite; there is no past and no future. All around this central point is the time and space of the world. The closer we come to this point in the center, the slower time seems to move.

Textbooks reviewing Einsteinian relativity often use examples of spaceships traveling close to the speed of light. The metaphysical explorer does not need to find a spaceship. She or he merely needs to dedicate time to an intensive inner voyage. In silence and solitude, time unfolds and a variety of strange worlds are encountered.

Some of these worlds are potentially frightening. They are populated with fantastic creatures that could not possibly be part of our own imagination. Where do they come from? "If they are part of my own mind, what kind of person am I to have these grotesque images in my head?" "Are these disgusting things I envision really my wishful thinking?" "Am I really so evil?" "When I see these faces and hear these voices, I feel I must be possessed!"

Carl Jung spent most of his life exploring the world of the unconscious. His insight regarding the strange visions we experience led him to postulate the idea of a collective unconscious—that each of us has universal archetypes within us that transcend our personal experience and tap into a pool of unknown dimension. Jung himself had a propensity for taking extensive retreats in his famous isolated tower. Anyone who commits to a personal retreat of ten days or more will likely become intimate with the collective unconscious. Visions arise in the domain of angelic beings, and we feel ecstatic; other visions drop us into the depths of the demonic realms, and we may be terrified by what we see.

In the last section of this book we will discuss angelic visions and see how under their influence we often erroneously conclude that we have attained a high level of consciousness. In this chapter we are going to explore demonic visions. But first we need to address an important question: Why do we prefer angelic to demonic visions?

The answer seems fairly obvious: Angels are nice and pretty, while demons are nasty and ugly. Who wants to have a ghoul for a friend if a cherub is available? Moreover, if we become like those whose company we keep, it would seem logical to espouse the higher qualities.

This answer reflects another paradox in the spiritual quest. Teachers often suggest that our associations are a major part of the spiritual path. We read in wisdom teachings: "Let your house be a meeting place for sages, sit in the dust of their feet; and drink in their words thirstily."[24] And again, "Distance yourself from a bad neighbor; do not associate with a wicked person. . . ."[25]

However, we need to remember the concept that demons and dark visions also have a spark of the divine and are useful in promoting spiritual development. Mircea Eliade points out that the task of demons is

. . . *precisely to kill the profane man, thus enabling him to be regenerated. . . . Demons were, among other things, the masters of initiation. They seized the neophytes, tortured them, subjected them to a great number of trials, and finally killed them in order that they might be reborn with a regenerated body and soul.*[26]

There are similarities between demonic visions and pain. Pain is not pleasant, and we do not welcome it, yet it plays a major role in the process of spiritual development—so too demonic visions. Nobody wants to be tortured and subjected to difficult trials, yet on the spiritual path we all seek some kind of initiation into expanded states of consciousness.

It is important to keep in mind that it is only our judgments—our likes and dislikes—that differentiate between angelic and demonic visions. We have preferences. The visions themselves are neither good nor bad. They are just visions. We may label them as weird or supernatural, beautiful or monstrous, sweet or sickening, but this is just a point of view. The truth of the experiences is that they are neutral. Hence, wanting angelic visions and hating demonic ones misses the point altogether. Indeed, we may be missing the specific element we need for spiritual growth by avoiding the dark side.

How do we deal with experiences that come from the shadow worlds? The fact that we do not particularly like these images will not prevent them from visiting us. The advice of the sages to associate with more refined spiritual beings is addressed to circumstances over which we have some control. Only a fool would summon evil as a guest; however, if a demon shows up uninvited at the dinner table, what do we do?

There are a number of approaches to this problem. Some are based on the widespread teaching that the individual is no match for the force of evil; the separate self will be vanquished like a mote of dust in the hurricane of evil's power. Some teachings engage evil through the insight of "what it really is," while others turn to the only source of power greater than evil, the divine Creator.

One approach under the category of naming evil for

what it really is follows the teaching that Satan is another word for *māyā,* illusion. The essence of satanic energy is deception—Satan is the liar *par excellence.* Almost everything we take in through the senses and virtually everything we think is colored by deception and illusion; this is why evil is so powerful. Indeed, anything that has the quality of comparison, duality, or contrast must be a misconception, for the ultimate truth is unity: oneness. Consequently, since the process of thinking operates by virtue of discrimination, thought must be illusory. This insight grows through meditation to the point where demonic visions are nothing more than different forms of illusion. When we have achieved this degree of awareness, visions from the dark side will no longer burden us.

Another technique following along the lines of understanding demons for what they really are is suggested by a modern psychological theory that our personality is composed of many characteristics, some of which we identify with, thinking of them as "I/me," and some of which we disown, thinking of them as "not I/me." These disowned parts find expression in many ways. As long as we fail to integrate them, they will often appear in our dreams (or meditations) as demons. Thus, demons really represent the disowned characteristics of our personality seeking recognition.[27]

A completely different approach is suggested in the traditional religious motif to "merge ourselves with the Divine." Many religious thinkers believe the purpose of evil is to drive us into the arms of our Creator. Our surrender and dissolution into the Divine Protector is sufficient to provide us with a degree of equanimity. This does not assume we will be safe from all harm, for that would be ego-oriented submission, not true egoless surrender. The attitude of someone who has completely surrendered is that what happens no longer matters. Even if harm is a consequence, it is God's will.

This position is nicely summed up in a statement by a nineteenth-century Christian writer named Voysey, quoted by William James:

> It is the experience of myriads of trustful souls, that this sense of God's unfailing presence with them in their going out and in their coming in, and by night and day, is a source of absolute repose and confident calmness. It drives away all fear of what may befall them. That nearness of God is a constant security against terror and anxiety. It is not that they are at all assured of physical safety, or deem themselves protected by a love which is denied to others, but that they are in a state of mind equally ready to be safe or to meet with injury. If injury befall them, they will be content to bear it because the Lord is their keeper, and nothing can befall them without his will. [28]

Another Christian method is in the advice offered by the anonymous author of *The Cloud of Unknowing*:

> If memories of your past actions keep coming between you and God, or any new thought or sinful impulse . . . you can use every "dodge," scheme, and spiritual stratagem you can find to put them away. These arts are better learned from God by experience, than from any human teacher. Try them out . . . act as if you did not know that they [sinful impulses, et cetera] were so strongly pushing in between you and God. . . . [or] When you feel you are completely powerless to put these thoughts away, cower down before them like some cringing captive overcome in battle. . . . In this way you surrender yourself to God . . . and this humility causes God himself to come down in his might . . . just as a father would act toward his child. [29]

The common denominator in all techniques, whether oriented to insight or surrender, is acceptance. When dark visions appear, resistance or aversion will only provide a playground for these forces. They feed on the repelling energy. It should be noted that they would also feed on attracting energy; therefore, welcoming them will also give them added strength. The only certain way of dealing with this power is to be neutral, neither to push it away nor entertain it.

The wisdom of the Christian Desert Fathers teaches:

*One of the elders said: It is not because evil thoughts come to us that we are condemned, but only because we make use of the evil thoughts. It can happen that from these thoughts we suffer shipwreck, but it can also happen that because of them we may be crowned.*[30]

It is a mistaken belief that the sages or enlightened beings rid themselves of callers from the Other Side. The darkness is a fact of life, just like day and night. Human beings must learn how to deal with the shadow side. We see, for example, in a story about the Baal Shem Tov:

*He said that angels were at the right hand of Jacob, our Patriarch, and demons were at his left hand. Angels were also on the right side of the Besht [another name for the Baal Shem Tov], and demons were on his left side. But he refused to use the angels because they were holy, and he refused to use the demons because they were liars.*[31]

We find in other stories that the Besht overpowered the dark side by invoking one of the names of God. His daily relationship, however, was neutral. The demons were always at his left side. Note that he did not turn to the angels, but treated them neutrally as well.

Thus, either through insight or clinging to God, we remain calm whenever we are faced with demonic visions. If we do not respond to them, they will dissipate in their own time. If we choose to understand them as disowned parts of our personality, we may gain greater harmony in our relationship to the world. But this often requires professional psychological counseling.

When psychological or spiritual counselors are not readily available, we can handle demonic visions on our own by merely observing them as a curiosity. Just let them come and let them go. In this way, they have no power over us and will visit us only occasionally rather than being a dominant part of our spiritual lives. In any case, they should not be resisted or viewed as a reflection of serious personal problems. They are normal experiences for all people. They help us grow on the spiritual path, and in many ways are a significant component of our internal guidance system.

# SEPARATION

We arrive at a retreat center, looking forward to a ten-day sit. We have some anxiety, since this is the first time we have ever taken a retreat like this. On the way here we have been thinking, "What is it going to be like? Will I be able to complete the retreat or will I make a fool of myself? I hope the teachers are good; I hope they are not too hard on us. I wonder what my room is going to be like? I hope the bed is comfortable." Our minds repeat all the details, worrying about our special needs and how we will be accepted.

Even before we walk through the door, we have ideas about the food, the temperature, the bugs, the meditation hall, the beds, the early wake-up, the exercise room, the bathroom, the showers. All our habits come into question. In addition, we have fantasized about the serenity, transcendence, equanimity, and joy we hope to find. "This could be the experience of my life; everything may change for the good after this."

This mixture of hope and fear has agitated us and we are nervous when we walk up to the registration desk. When we finally get to our assigned room, we may be grateful for some of its amenities, but we quickly begin examining its deficiencies. We judge everything—and thereby make it not "me." "Wait a minute, this bed is too hard. These blankets are too rough. I see a spider in the corner; oh no, I hate spiders. The window is facing north. That means there will not be much light, and I am going to be cold. The closet is awfully small. This will never do."

We walk up and down the hall, peeking into other rooms. "Here is one that is bigger, but it is right next to the bathroom and it will be noisy. This one has great blankets, and the bed is perfect, but the room is so cramped, I would hardly be able to move around. Here is one with a gorgeous view; oh, but this is for two people." We assess and compare all the good and bad points of the different rooms and make up a mental list of the rooms better than ours.

Now our minds begin to build a new tension. "Should I go to the registration desk and ask for a new room assignment? Things will be so much better if I have another room. This is going to be a hard retreat, I should make myself as comfortable as possible. At least I should run down to the other rooms and switch blankets, trade heaters, take that nice vase I saw to keep flowers in my room, get a better towel, find some curtains."

Notice how big the "I/me" has been up to this point. "I want things my way, I have habits and needs." Throughout all this internal dialogue, we maintain a constant process of identifying who we think we are. "If I did not have these habits and needs, who would I be anyway? I know who I am, what my preferences are, what makes me feel good and what makes me miserable. I know what has worked for me in the past, and I assume the same will be true in the future. I can be flexible about some things, but some I really want to have my way."

The judging mind works constantly. Usually, it defines "I/me" by pushing away what is not "I/me." As long as we can judge something, we have a sense of ourselves, we give definition to our self. When we are told there are no other beds, we either compromise and accept this bed as ours, in which case we no longer think of it; or the bed becomes a major, lumpy problem in our lives. Our judgment may then be transformed into aversion and perhaps hatred. Unless we come to terms with it, the bed can now dominate our thoughts and ruin our entire retreat.

All of this gives us a strong sense of ourselves. When we are not judging, we are comparing. "This room is bigger than mine, or smaller; it is lighter, or darker; it is warmer, or cooler. That person sits better than I do, that other person is so much better dressed than I am. We meditators are better people than the rest of the world; we are more serious, work harder, deserve more spiritual rewards." This judging and comparing goes on constantly.

Most of us live in a state of "hard mind." This is caused by false discrimination, which forms a shell of separation. The mind's natural function is to discriminate. On the most essential level, all our senses require discrimination. We share this with a large part of animal life. The higher level of human discrimination is intrinsic to conceptual thought, values, and ideals and is the essential element in all spiritual endeavor. Up to this point, discrimination is the greatest gift we have, for it allows our minds to work.

As with many affairs in life, our greatest assets often turn out to be our greatest liabilities. When discrimination is used selflessly, as an abstract function that allows cognition, it is the necessary ingredient for exploration into the meaning and purpose of life. When the self steps in, it uses discrimination as its instrument of survival.

The survival mechanism of self-identity is the implacable enemy of unity, acceptance, and surrender, for these qualities destroy the sense of self. This mechanism of self-"survival" uses our power of discrimination to differentiate, categorize, and separate everything from the (illusory) initial idea of the self as a unique entity.

Judging and comparing are useful modes of thought when they are not reinforcing our self-image. We can judge whether or not a film or book is worthwhile material to share with our children; we can judge whether an unusual expense is worth invading the budget. We can compare courses of education or spiritual paths.

Most of the time, however, when we slow ourselves down and observe our mental processes, our judging and comparing minds are filled with meaningless trivia. This is nothing more than an attempt to separate us from the rest of the world. An early surprise in store for spiritual aspirants is awareness of the amazing degree to which our minds judge and criticize almost everything that is going on.

On a group retreat, this "hard mind" first assesses the way the conditions are set up. The accommodations, the schedule, the efficiency of the staff—nothing is done just right. After a while, our judging mind finds faults in all the other people on this retreat. Whether sitting, walking, eating, dressing, or breathing, everyone does something wrong. There may also be one or two who appear to do everything right, and our comparing mind may find that depressing. They make us feel bad; they sit so still and look so good.

Later on during the retreat, since we have not yet reached enlightenment, we conclude that there must be something wrong with the teachers. "They talk too much or too little; they do not pay enough attention; they do not really care; they are fakes; what gives them the right to call themselves teachers anyway!"

When alone, the dialogue of hard mind often turns inward. "I am not as ready now as I was last week. I am not trying hard enough. If only so-and-so had not done such-and-such, I would be in a much better frame of mind. It's all their fault. My last retreat was better, quieter, calmer. Today is a lousy day. I'm getting no-where."

These are thoughts of alienation. The shell of hard mind protects our sense of self by judging and comparing all stimuli, identifying things as not "me," and thereby keeping "I/me" safe. If we take a peek inside the shell, there is nobody home. Indeed, the shell itself gives the impression that it is protecting something. Our whole sense of what the shell is protecting comes from the shell itself. A large percentage of who we think we are is dependent upon what we think we are not. In the end, what is inside the shell?

If we ask ourselves who we are, what do we describe? A name? Are we just names, addresses, or telephone numbers? Are we occupations or body descriptions? Are we a combination of likes and dislikes, or could we adequately describe ourselves in terms of relationships? In fact, it is impossible to get a substantive description of ourselves. Even a distinctive ear shape, voice, fingerprint, or DNA code is not sufficient. This measurement can separate us from the rest of humanity, but the proof that we are distinct individuals does not inform us who we are—it only gives us details, by comparing with others, of what we are not.

The deeper we look, the more we realize how little we are able to specify who we are. Some teachers have as their major practice the question "Who am I?" This question leads to a vital insight: We discover that all along we have been pretending that we exist by defining everything that we are not. An insight such as this comes only through direct experience. It is not something we can learn from a book.

Meanwhile, how do we work with the unpleasant mind state of hardness, alienation, and separation? In our daily lives, we are so accustomed to this frame of mind we assume it is the only way to live. As we become increasingly sensitive to our thought patterns, we come to the painful realization that our judging minds are constantly knocking down everybody around us in order to build ourselves up. We may be discouraged to observe the baseness of our own thoughts as our imaginations rip apart people who have not even looked at us, much less mistreated us.

If our minds behave this way when nothing is threatening us, what happens when we believe we are being harmed? Our hard minds can close us in so tightly that we become rocks in our attitude toward the individual we believe is out to injure us, and we may become hostile toward the entire world. If this happens on a retreat, our meditation is seriously affected, we become estranged from everyone around us—even the food begins to taste terrible.

A hard mind affects our whole state of being. When we are in a positive mind state, we enter situations in an open attitude. If we approach the identical situation with a tight mind, criticism, judgment, and comparison arise. This is what is meant by separation. It has nothing to do with our physical relationship to the world; rather, spiritual separation is related to our perspective.

We see this clearly as our minds flip from one criticism

to the next, from one comparison to another. It does not matter what we are comparing or judging, as long as we are able to do so without restriction. In the aspect of separation, we always have a subject for our critical minds; separation is a self-perpetuating process.

A good cure for the hard mind syndrome is the retreat experience itself. An environment of silence clears away all the normal distractions of life and critical thoughts become so obvious, they cannot be ignored. Indeed, these thoughts arise so frequently, they become obnoxious and this helps initiate the insight that slowly liberates us from the grip of our hard minds.

In our growing consciousness, we recognize thoughts for what they are, and we begin to see their ephemeral quality. Nothing persists as we move from subject to subject. As a new negative thought arises, the current one disappears. This continuous dance of the colored veils of criticism and alienation filters everything so that we are unable to see things as they are; rather we see only reflected hues. However, a spiritual retreat will not allow us to abandon the true nature of creation for long and thus we begin to suspect all appearances.

This does not mean that our minds will be brought into line instantly. We are firmly habituated in a negative process of thinking, and it will continue for a long time to come. But with practice, we do begin to place our thoughts in their proper perspective, recognizing that they are usually a result of our search for identity rather than a reflection of reality. This causes the negativity to become less dominant and our mind state automatically softens.

Consequently, the key to dealing with a hard mind is recognizing it for what it is. As with all aversions, if our hard mind state is the focus of aversion, if we try to push it away, we feed this negative energy and it will continue to trouble us. Therefore, we must not be too severe with ourselves when we realize we are judging others. Criticism of others is destructive enough for our well-being, but when we focus the sharpness of our critical minds upon ourselves, the result can be devastating.

Self-criticism is the most perverse expression of our judgmental minds. We initially built a false identity through our judgments about and comparisons with others, and now we attack this false self-identity by judging ourselves. This leads to an *Alice in Wonderland* scenario. It is like a dog looking in the mirror and perceiving itself as a cat. The dog begins to chase its own tail, thinking it is chasing a cat. However, while engaged in the chase, it *feels* like a dog because chasing cats is what dogs do.

Another part of the dog feels itself being chased. It feels that if it is being chased, it must be a cat. Each part identifies with the experience of chasing or being chased. That the chase is based on a magical mirror of illusion is not relevant, but that the chase is occurring at all infers substance.

We judge others. This gives us a sense of self-identity. As long as we judge others, the self-identity—the "dog"—is substantiated because the judgment is like the chase. Once self-judging begins, the self-identity gets confused and begins to see itself as a "cat" because now it is being chased. The wonderland we live in accepts dogs chasing cats as a matter of fact; if we did not, our self-identity would immediately vanish.

Self-judgment can lead to a belief that we are worthless because we always fall short when we judge ourselves. Just as something thought it was a cat because it was being chased, we think ourselves worthless because of the

UNPLEASANT MIND STATES

experience of constant self-criticism. Yet, the criticism may continue because the part criticizing also gets identity, feeling like a dog because it is involved in a chase. This is the perversion of self-criticism.

The hard mind of separation is centered in the ego. Our egos cannot exist without a sense of separation. This is a crucial point. Until we gain direct experience of what this separation costs, our natural inclination is constantly to judge, criticize, and compare in order to maintain the sense of separateness. As our awareness expands, we judge ourselves and others less, we soften, and the sense of unity grows. The hallmarks of a mystic are oceanic consciousness, universal perspective, and open-mindedness. Judging, criticizing, and comparing falls away, except where it is appropriate for the ongoing enlightenment process.

Working to soften our hard minds and constricted thoughts is one arena where we can make rapid progress in the early stages of spiritual development. Most of our judgments have so little substance that we do not require a great deal of internal light to realize the truth about them. Our first seven- or ten-day retreat will often support growth in this area, which in itself makes the retreat worthwhile. A significant step in gaining insight on the nature of the mind is achieved when we break the self-sustaining nature of a constricted thought process.

We have already considered different types of spiritual impediments caused by self-identification. We have seen the natural progression of desire into greed or aversion into hatred. We have noted the constant mental interruptions in our practice, the busy mind that is related to a sense of selfness. We have touched upon the need for surrender and the process of dissolving into the unity. Every tradition deals with these questions in its own way, but most agree that the primary task for true spiritual progress necessitates relinquishing our sense of self. Yet, the part of ourselves we call "I/me" seems to be so enormous and so tenacious that the prospect of it melting away appears almost impossible.

As we gain more experience in meditation, we come to an amazing insight. We become aware of a basic teaching we have often read about, but which we really cannot appreciate until we have direct experience. In its simplest form, the teaching is: *there is no "I/me"!* When we slow ourselves down in meditation, and especially on retreat, we are able to come closer and closer to the timeless instant called NOW.

It is important to realize that what we call a moment, what we normally call "now," is not the spiritual NOW to which teachers refer. Our idea of a moment is still caught in the web of time. We could measure a moment in terms of milliseconds, or even less, but it remains somehow measurable. When we get to NOW, we have nothing to measure, because it is timeless. There was nothing prior to NOW, and nothing comes after it. It is always NOW.

This teaching has become commonplace, but it remains an enigmatic lesson most of humanity has yet to learn. As NOW is infinite, it means we have no separation, no sense of self. When our practice slows us down and opens us to NOW consciousness, we develop the insight that our identity with "I/me" is constantly melting away, effortlessly.

The full experience of the insight that our primal, natural state of being does not include a sense of ego-identity is a major enlightenment experience—a shocking realization so mind-shattering that it usually transforms the individual forever. It is this: Although we often engage in strenuous spiritual practices to break down our self-identity and we think we are struggling mightily to be at one with the Divine, in truth the veils of separation are constantly vanishing—they too are illusions. We need not work to remove them, *the veils fall away by themselves!* However, the instant one vanishes, another appears. If the new veil did not appear, we would immediately realize our natural state, which is always in the NOW!

But if this is so, why are we not all enlightened? If it is normal for the veils to vanish automatically, and this is our natural enlightened state, then every new veil would also fall away and we would always be in the NOW.

Then comes the truth—an extraordinary realization. We discover that what is really happening is that as the illusion of self begins to fall, we scurry desperately to brace up the facade. The instant a veil falls away, we rush into the breach to throw up more clouds and veils so as not to see the true nature of things!

This is hard to believe. It means that we are only paying lip service to our aspiration to be at one with God, to be liberated from our delusions, and to be at peace with ourselves and the world. Yet the truth is that we have such a deep terror of eliminating our sense of identity that we are constantly engaged in building an edifice that gives us a feeling of security. Although the facade crumbles from instant to instant, our internal armies stand by to prop up anything we can cling to, so that we do not disappear into the NOW, which is always standing here ready to take us.

If we reflected on our thoughts as we came to the retreat center, we were worried about how our needs were going to be met. In psychological terms, it is the natural anxiety of entering the unknown. Not many people walk into an entirely new situation without deliberation, testing the way, maintaining as much control as possible. Our primitive survival mechanism gives us appropriate warnings and cautions when entering new, potentially dangerous situations. A primary characteristic of familiar situations is that they are safe—we know what to expect and can thereby plan. The unknown is dangerous; we have no way to prepare for contingencies.

This essential survival mechanism is at the center of our fear of the NOW. We know the world of time and space, we are familiar with how things work in this world. The world of NOW, however, is completely unknown and unknowable. It is always spontaneous, it can never be controlled. Entering the NOW is diametrically in opposition to every consideration of personal survival.

What a shock to discover that most of us are actually *afraid* of being enlightened! If survival is our root instinct, the fear is well founded. Once we no longer have the props by which we define ourselves, our mundane self-perception ceases to exist. At that stage, who do we see in the mirror? This is a key point to ponder; it lies at the heart of stillness. If we are unaware of our primal fear of enlightenment, we can spend a lifetime chasing apparitions.

# AGITATION AND FATIGUE

Once a retreat has begun, meditators often experience extreme shifts in energy. Some people become so charged with vitality they have trouble sleeping and their minds race wildly. In this state, we often find concentration difficult and sitting still a slow torture. We experience an intense flow of ideas, a sheer torrent of thought. This agitation is characterized by a lack of continuity; an incessant shifting and vacillating mental process persists without a common thread.

At the other extreme, soon after a retreat begins, we may experience a wave of exhaustion sweeping over us and every move costs great effort. The mind becomes so sluggish that we have no strength for any level of concentration. After a few minutes of sitting, our heads drop forward or our bodies lean over and sleep seems to be the only possible alternative. Indeed, sleep seems so imperative that we feel as though our survival depends upon it.

We all experience periods of nervousness or fatigue, but on retreat these qualities intensify. Meditation accentuates experiences because the stillness is in distinct contrast to our normal lives. In addition, when we have no distractions, the experiences of agitation or fatigue can more fully run their courses and thereby express themselves more dramatically. A third explanation is more esoteric. Some teachers have suggested that meritorious spiritual effort always engenders great resistance. If we allow the resistance to overwhelm us, we will fall back to a lower level in our spiritual progress. If we recognize that the resistance is a gift, we will understand that the strength we must develop to overcome barriers has its source in higher consciousness. Resistance is an incentive to spiritual growth.

Whatever the reason, when we experience agitation during an intense retreat, we sometimes think we are going crazy. The wild motion of the mind resembles a hurricane or typhoon at sea. Great surges of emotion may break over us; one minute we have a feeling of despair, the next moment we rise with uncontrollable elation. We bob like a cork in confused breakers, shoved this way and that. If we were not on retreat, we would probably call a doctor.

A similar extreme can be experienced with fatigue. In Buddhist literature, fatigue is characterized as "sloth and torpor." This is an accurate description of the ordeal. We move in a sea of glue and the mind feels as though it has coagulated. After sleeping for a number of hours, we awaken, go to the bathroom, get a cup of tea, and then feel ready for a nap. On some retreats, we sleep almost all the time for the first three or four days. We may attempt a few sits and try to eat each day, but sleep can take up eighteen to twenty hours.

Obviously something exceptional is happening on retreat. Just as the physical body has a basic metabolism, the spiritual body also has a form of metabolism. When we sit quietly and begin to concentrate, this releases an abundance of energy that is normally used in discursive thought and physical engagement with the world. The result is like giving a plate of food to a starving person. If

UNPLEASANT MIND STATES

he or she eats too quickly, it can cause severe illness and even death.

Our physical metabolism adjusts slowly to environmental conditions. The kind of work we do, the food we eat, the exercise we take, and the weather outside affect our basic metabolism. We understand the need for physical nourishment and usually we do what is necessary to meet these biological demands.

Unfortunately, most of us starve our spiritual body—we are ignorant of its needs. Its demands are expressed so subtly that we are frequently too busy to pay attention. Therefore, our spiritual metabolism is often like a flickering candle. It flares, sputters, and dims on the edge of self-extinction, but as long as we are alive, it somehow survives.

The spiritual metabolism can make a remarkable recovery with just minimal nourishment. One line in a book, one glance at nature, one moment at an inspiring event, and the candle will flame brightly for a little while. Then the old patterns usually close in and more sputtering ensues.

A spiritual retreat is much more than minimal nourishment. It is a grand feast. Thus, we sometimes have an experience analogous to the story of two guests who attend a banquet. When they approach the banquet table, they find it filled with an amazing variety of delights. One guest flits from dish to dish, having a wonderful time, not knowing what to take next—the variety of choice is overwhelming. This guest never really enjoys himself because he is constantly on the move, bewildered by the array. The other guest enters, stops at the first dish and proceeds to eat too much. He remains unaware of the rest of the banquet. His dish is so rich and filling that he soon gets sick and must leave.

The experience of agitation, running from dish to dish, occurs at various times during a retreat. This should not be confused with our normal level of thinking. It is more like hyper-thinking. This state may be sparked by various circumstances, all apparently innocuous. We may begin to ponder an idea that seems important; we may notice a simple message on the bulletin board; or there may be no apparent initial cause. Suddenly we realize our minds are racing on ten tracks at once. We may have a few moments to observe our feeling of tension, but we are soon overwhelmed by fleeting thoughts in wild disarray.

When this occurs, we must simply wait it out. The strategy is not much different, except in degree, from contending with ordinary thinking when we are trying to meditate. The agitated mind disturbs us because the thoughts are much more turbulent and feel out of control. Yet agitation does not usually have a long life. Its own energy tends to burn out. Steadiness in practice is the remedy for an active mind. Sooner or later, the mind will calm down.

Fatigue is a much more insidious problem, taking many different forms. It can be the overwhelming fatigue people often experience at the beginning of a retreat or the lingering variety, which appears at different times later on. Some people find the first sit in the morning exceptionally burdensome. Waking up so early is difficult for them. Others have a problem with the last sit at night or directly after a meal. Many are plagued by sleepiness throughout the day.

At the beginning of a retreat we can find many rationales for fatigue. People often arrive exhausted. They need a few days to gather themselves and this may involve physical recuperation. This kind of sleepiness is not really what we are talking about. Still, it is important to note because we need to be prepared for a period of transition. If this is a retreat of ten days or less, we should consider the possibility of taking it easy a few days beforehand so that the first days are not completely lost in sleep.

If we were going to Paris, the Caribbean, or anywhere else exciting on a week's vacation, even if we arrived physically wiped out, after sleeping late for a day we would be out exploring and would not let sleep interfere with the rest of the week. The main reason is that on vacation we are interested in what we are doing.

Only a fraction of the fatigue we experience on retreat is due to physical need. Most of it is the result of continuing spiritual metabolic readjustment. There are a number of methods for dealing with this. My own inclination is to be somewhat self-indulgent during the first couple of days of a retreat. I let myself nap more often. But I nap only for short periods—my alarm is always set. Twenty minutes is the maximum time I allow myself, sometimes only ten or fifteen minutes. I have found that a short nap can be refreshing; however, anything over twenty minutes can leave me groggy for the rest of the day.

After a few days, any fatigue is almost certainly a spiritual rather than physical need. Some teachers believe that we are not overcome by sleep itself, but by the desire to sleep. The most useful method for dealing with this desire is to recognize that the feeling of drowsiness will pass in its own time. Ram Dass wrote about his own experience with fatigue:

> Fatigue . . . was a chronic problem for me. I remember propping myself up with piles of cushions so that I would not fall over into sleep. I often went to meditation courses because I was afraid that alone I would drift off into sleep. I've since learned to handle drowsy

*states with breathing techniques. What I experienced as fatigue often was actually a state of deep stillness that I misinterpreted. Instead of taking the feeling of fatigue as an invitation for a nap, I now regard it as a passing state, and keep sitting.*[32]

Our normal reaction when we feel hunger is to eat something, but if we wait awhile, the hunger will pass. We often find drowsiness especially pressing and difficult to resist when we are sitting quietly, without distraction. Yet, this feeling too will pass. We get stronger in dealing with our reactions as we recondition ourselves. At first, drowsiness is a signal that demands the response of lying down. After a while, it is just another state of mind.

The mind states of agitation and fatigue are major hindrances we face in the development of one-pointed concentration. Buddhists list five such hindrances, the other three being desire, aversion, and doubt. The hindrances come and go, uninvited, as part of our normal mental experience.

These mental states are troublesome mainly because we tend to identify with them. It makes a big difference whether we think "I am tired," rather than "There is tiredness." If we identify with the tiredness, we have a tendency to proceed to "Why am I always so tired?" or "What is wrong with me that I should feel so tired?" If we are not identified with the fatigue, then we do not have to take it personally. We do not have to connect an "I/me" with the feeling of fatigue, we do not have to question it; fatigue is merely a state of mind.

Once we are past the initial stage of a retreat that may require more resting time, we need to make a special effort when the signals of fatigue arise. Fatigue is more seductive than most unpleasant mind states, because a relationship exists between strength of mind and effort. The feeling of fatigue is a sense of weakness. We convince ourselves that we do not have the strength to make any effort. However, if we were able to turn on a television or go to a movie, we would become instantly alert. Why is this? Our alertness is sharpened because we are interested in what is going on. Interest is always an important element in effort.

Teachers use different tactics to arouse interest. One method is to use our natural fear to combat sleepiness. We all know that a person needs to fight sleepiness when caught outside in a snowstorm because of the possibility that he will never awaken. The same argument is used as advice against giving in to fatigue during spiritual practice.

Philip Kapleau writes:

> Dozing off, at any time of day, is a common complaint of sitters. It doesn't appear to be related to whether you are tired or rested or have had your normal amount of sleep or not, the problem is one of motivation. . . . What you need to do is remind yourself, when dozing off, that death may come at any time, and that to have the rare opportunity of being born a human being in this lifetime and not to realize your True-Nature is, as one master put it, to have lived in vain.[33]

Ramana Maharshi approaches sleepiness as just another thought. He advises bringing moderation into our lives in all matters.

> We should not sleep too much or go without it altogether, but sleep only moderately. To prevent too much sleep, we must try to have no thoughts or chalana [movement of the mind], we must eat only sattvic food [fresh fruits and vegetables, dairy, and grains], and that only in moderate measure, and not indulge in too much physical activity. The more we control thought, activity, and food the more we shall be able to control sleep.[34]

Many teachings suggest that cutting back on sleep is an important part of practice. Sleep deprivation rapidly induces altered mind states. Also, when we are in such a state, we often need much less sleep. Many people on long, intensive retreats require no more than four hours of sleep a night. This is due to the combination of reduced physical activity, less stress, and the benefits of deep meditation. We can continue for many weeks of minimal sleep without feeling the slightest sense of fatigue. Thus, by actually reducing the amount of sleep, the retreatant soon discovers that less sleep is needed.

Some Buddhist retreats require cutting back the sleeping schedule immediately to five hours a night. This is gradually reduced to three or four hours sleep each night. The Sufis battle the *nafs* (the base instincts) by drastically reducing both food and sleep. They fast all day, eating only at night, and perform practices to stay awake most of the night.

> Lack of sleep was considered one of the most effective means on the mystical Path. . . . Many of the mystics would avoid stretching out their legs or lying down when slumber overcame them, for all of them hoped for some revelation after the long nights of sleeplessness, which extended over years, if we can believe the sources.[35]

A well-known Sufi tale describes a man who did not sleep for forty years, but who was eventually overcome by sleep. In this sleep he finally saw God, and exclaimed: "Oh Lord, I was seeking you in nightly vigils, but I have found you in sleep!" God answered: "Oh Shah, you found Me by means of those nightly vigils; if you had not sought Me there, you would not have found Me here."[36]

Whether we are novices or advanced retreatants, agitation and fatigue are common mind states experienced on retreat. And, like other mental states, they come and

UNPLEASANT MIND STATES

go. Experience teaches us to observe them while continuing to concentrate on the main focus of our meditation. In this way, we will begin to understand their nature, and we will be able to deal with them more effectively each time they arise.

# DOUBT

Spiritual endeavor is always grounded in faith. This should not be the blind faith of fanaticism, but rather the part of us that believes there is something more to life than randomness. This faith helps us follow an unknown path, allows us to continue in mysterious dimensions, and encourages us to persist even though there is no tangible goal.

Doubt is the handmaiden of the skeptical intellect; it is the most treacherous negative mind state for any spiritual aspirant. Doubt constantly jabs at us, seeking vulnerable points, trying to break us. Sometimes it seems to lurk in every corner; at others it remains hidden for a long period and then reappears in a sudden, devastating manner. Everyone on the spiritual path has faced serious misgivings and gone through crises that were shaped by doubt. These crises can be quite severe.

Uncertainty is often coupled with other unpleasant mind states. With aversion, we are afraid that the experience will never end. With pain, we believe that we are never going to be healthy again. With fear, we may be apprehensive of impending death. Demonic visions cause us to question our sanity; the feeling of separateness makes us skeptical that we will ever have peace; fatigue causes us to wonder if we will ever again have strength.

Every unpleasant mind state ultimately uses doubt to break our resistance.

When doubt stands on its own, it can be even more terrifying. We may become skeptical that anything transcends the mundane, endless suffering of life. We hear it in the lamenting song "Is That All There Is?" We may distrust the idea that we can reach another state of consciousness, even that such a level exists. Or, we believe that we do not deserve it, our lives are too filled with corrupt thoughts, and that we are worthless, helpless creatures. Also, we may have reservations that spiritual traditions and teachers really teach us anything. They are not enlightened, they play on fear, they manipulate us for their own selfish needs. Perhaps saddest of all is the doubt that there is any truth, everything is relative, and we have no way to determine good and bad, right and wrong; we believe ethics are ultimately irrelevant.

In Judaism, doubt is viewed as one of the greatest enemies of the tradition. When the Hebrew nation made its exodus from Egypt, the first adversary it encountered in the new land was the kingdom of Amalek. The people following Moses were commanded by God not to be satisfied merely with the defeat of this kingdom, but to destroy everything associated with Amalek. Many scholars would later wonder why this decree was so harsh, but Kabbalists explained that the name Amalek equals the Hebrew word *suffek,* which means doubt.[37] In other words, the Hebrews were being instructed by God, so to speak, that they must eradicate any remnant of uncertainty if they were to maintain faith when facing the ordeal ahead of them.

Even the earliest and smallest doubts must not be given a foothold in one's mind. They can and will rapidly grow into a fearsome opponent that may defeat us. This foe conquers us by weakening our will, destroying our hope, and casting us into jaws of despair. It is subtle and insidious; many teachers tell us we must be ruthless in eradicating it.

Compassion and loving kindness are essential traits on the spiritual path, but there are also times when we must be completely without compassion. The destruction of small, nagging doubts is one of these times. In modern terms, we could use the example of having compassion for a single cancer cell. If compassion were our sole guiding principle, we might let the poor orphan survive. But common sense tells us that when we cut out a malignant growth, we must not allow even one small cancer cell to remain behind.

Doubt is truly the cancer of spiritual development. It may begin as a small, harmless question in our consciousness, such as "Does this retreat process really work?" Over time it can mushroom into "This is totally stupid," and even, "If I do not get out of this place, I'm going to go crazy!"

Yet, as with all the negative mind states, suspicion does play an important role. Perhaps we are genuinely in a dangerous situation and really need to get out of that place. Thus the question arises: How do we determine when our misgivings are simply a passing negative state of mind and when they are valid caution signs?

This is a classic question. We are taught that a disciple must surrender heart and soul to a teacher. It is all well and good to surrender if the teacher is a true teacher, but what if the teacher is a fake? What if somewhere along the way this teacher asks us to jump off a cliff? As we reach the precipice, apprehension will certainly step in. How will we know whether it is really protecting us or if it is keeping us from the ultimate realization?

These decisions are not easy. We are often presented with such precipices. For example, we may reach what we think are limits of pain, or we may encounter fear that is extremely threatening. Most of the time we need to jump, but sometimes we need to turn away. How do we know what to do and when to do it?

The essential power of doubt is the unknown; it cannot exist in the face of truth—one is diametrically opposed to the other. The unknown is a territory where truth is hidden. Thus every time we step into the unknown, we encounter doubt at its fullest intensity. Standing at a precipice, the unknown a vast chasm before us, we may conjure up vivid images of permanent injury and pull back to safety. Or we may be whipped forward, encouraged to jump now or forever lose the chance. We vacillate, not knowing which impulse to trust.

One solution is to let go of the issue at hand and become immersed in the indecision itself. "What is pushing me to jump? What does it want, what motivates it, what are its expectations? What is holding me back? What is it afraid of? What is the heart of my fear?" In this method, our vacillation becomes the focus of our meditation and this defuses the tension of the precipice. No longer caught in indecision, we are able to explore our mental processes, and out of this may come insight.

This method assumes it is safer not to jump if we have serious reservations. There will be many opportunities to face the precipice in the future. Until we develop a more intimate understanding of our doubting nature and come to appreciate it through direct experience, we should not diminish the possibility that our reservations may indeed be an important and valid warning.

The other method is to develop and strengthen our faith. Traditions with a godhead have faith in the omnipotence of God; Buddhism has faith in the teachings of the Buddha, a scientist has faith in the laws of science. Faith obviously follows a different path from intellectual reason; it provides a foundation for most of our thoughts, feelings, and actions.

Although William James was referring to faith in God, he made an interesting observation about faith in general when he wrote:

> *Without regard to the question of their "truth," we are obliged, on account of their [the faith-states'] extraordinary influence upon action and endurance, to class them [faith-states] amongst the most important biological functions of mankind.*[38]

He went on to quote a Dr. Leuba, who asserted that humankind *uses* God and is empowered by the *belief in God;* this itself is our reality and it does not matter that God remains unknown and not understood.

Therefore, according to this premise, if we wish to deepen our faith in God, we do not need to have proof of the existence of God; we need only to read more inspirational texts and spend more time in devotional activities. Out of this, greater faith will naturally develop.

As our faith grows deeper, we accumulate the strength to deal with doubts when they arise. We develop a reservoir of willpower and inner security that protects us from the assault of doubt. Once the inner foundations built on faith are firm enough, we will find the courage to leap into the darkness. The successful act of leaping and surviving adds considerably to our faith. Our increased faith inhibits doubt and we begin flying off one cliff after another, until cliffs are no longer a challenge. Then we will be faced with a fresh challenge, a new level of doubt, and the progression will renew itself as we strive for ever higher levels of consciousness.

Eventually, when our faith is deep enough, one aspect of doubt becomes our ally. In Zen, this is a questioning level called *daigidan*. In the words of Yasutani, Philip Kapleau's teacher, *daigidan* is

> . . . *not a simple doubt, mind you, but a "doubt-mass"—and this inevitably stems from strong faith. It is a doubt as to why we and the world should appear so imperfect, so full of anxiety, strife, and suffering, when in fact our deep faith tells us exactly the opposite is true. It is a doubt which leaves us no rest.*[39]

At this point questioning drives us toward greater understanding. Since we believe that life does not have to be as terrible as it seems, there must be a way out of this predicament. We doubt that we need to be stuck and this adds fuel to our effort.

Although we may reach a level of faith that turns some uncertainty into an ally, we will still find the enemy lurking, waiting for a weak moment to pounce. As long as we have our intellect, there is the potential for distrust and suspicion. This is why it is important for us to recognize doubt before it carries us off into its own world of rejection and spiritual angst.

Rebbe Nachman of Breslov tells a wonderful story called "The Clever Man and the Simple Man." The clever man doubted everything and the simple man was a man of faith. Over the years the one increased his doubt while the other increased his faith. At one point in the story the clever man is seeking justice for having suffered a beating. Why was he beaten? "Because I was talking about the Baal Shem," he replied.[40] "I said that he was a liar and that the whole thing is nothing more than a big swindle."

The simple man is astonished that the other cannot perceive the specialness of the holy rabbi. Nonetheless, he

DOUBT

gives the clever man some new clothes and invites him to dine. At dinner the clever man remarks that there is no king. "What are you saying?" cries the simple man. "I have seen the king myself!"

"How do you know that he is the king?" answers his guest with a laugh. "Do you know him, and his father and his grandfather who were also kings? How do you know now that he really is the king? People told you that he was the king but they deceive you."[41]

This is the kind of doubt that occurs when the intellect becomes all-powerful. Then our world is so enclosed that simple truths are no longer accepted. The story goes on to describe how someone came and told the two men that the devil was looking for them. The simple man became afraid and prepared to run to the Baal Shem Tov for protection while the clever man said, "Do you really believe there is a devil?"

"If not, then who sent for us?" asked the simple man.

"It must be my brother," answered the clever man. "He wants to see me and made up the whole story."

The story continues. Every time the simple man states a fact, the clever man refutes it and invents a new answer.

In the end, the clever man finds himself in "a swamp filled with dirt and lime, and there in the middle of it sat the devil on a throne. The mud was as thick as glue." Still, this reality did not matter to the clever one. He cried out, "Villains! Why are you tormenting me? There is no such thing as the devil. You are just scoundrels. . . ."[42]

Rebbe Nachman tells us that the clever man remained in this mud pit for several years denying everything. One day the Baal Shem Tov came along and got him out of the pit and only then did the direct experience bring home the message.

If we open our eyes, we may discover that we also are

clever, and we too may be stuck in the thick mud of preconceptions. Our lives are filled with doubt, which we misconstrue as clear thinking. When we accept retreat discipline, we confront doubt head-on and this engagement inevitably softens us, opening us to new possibilities and different realities. We begin to gain a deeper faith and this is the springboard to growing awareness and spiritual insight.

The simple truth is that we must always persevere in our efforts toward enlightenment, never give up, never allow doubt a final victory. We may lose a skirmish here and there, but the secret of success is determination. Once we recognize that the enlightenment process has its ups and downs, and we realize it is not what we thought it was, then we are empowered by faith and not even doubt can stand up to this force of conviction. At the core of our resolve is enlightenment itself. We are certain to win, if we persist.

# PLEASANT MIND
# STATES

# INTRODUCTION

Now that we have explored so many unattractive mind states commonly experienced by retreatants, we may be wondering again about the question asked at the beginning of this book: Why in the world are people willing to undertake a process with so much potential for discomfort? Why do intelligent people keep coming back for more, especially when there is no guarantee of attainment? We do not receive a diploma after four years of sitting and there are no advanced degrees for meditators.

Obviously, millions of people have a strong motivation to engage and transcend powerful negative forces in the quest for illumination. As we saw earlier, the analogy of mountain climbing is often used. In order to succeed, a climber needs to be trained, healthy, in good spirits, and well equipped, which parallels the requirements of the spiritual path: purification, concentration, effort, and mastery. Often, the climb itself has an element of pleasure, but most of it is pure hard work. There may be rewards along a mountain trail and the end of each day may bring a sense of satisfaction, yet, as time goes on, the climbing becomes more demanding. The path becomes steep and at times treacherous.

When a summit is reached, the climber is rewarded with a "peak" experience. This idea of peak experience is a lovely concept. It means that we have reached a peak as a culmination of our effort and we also experience an emotional peak; in addition, we may be said to take a peek into another reality. This serves not just as a reward, but as motivation for the next round. Each time we reach the top of a mountain, new challenges ahead are revealed.

On these spiritual mountain paths, we frequently find signs left by travelers indicating which peaks are false and which are authentic. A false peak is often surrounded by clouds of pleasure. We may think we are standing on top of the world, but when the weather clears, we find that we are only on an outcrop and the trail upward continues a few steps away.

We will investigate some of the false peaks of the spiritual path in this section of the book. We will also explore authentic peaks, such as "tranquillity" or "equanimity," each of which has been mastered on many spiritual expeditions. Other peaks are much more rarely experienced, such as divine inspiration or union with God. Finally, on a clear day, we may be able to see the exceptional pinnacle of cosmic consciousness standing majestically in the distance. A few brave souls have scaled those heights, but the trails cannot be found on any charts.

Even before we reach the first peak, we may experience pleasurable states. The effort of climbing can induce a state of mild rapture that revitalizes and stimulates us. We may glimpse beautiful images in our meditation and uncover new sensitivity in our perception of nature. In these moments everything in creation appears to be in harmony.

However, if we begin to enjoy this rapture instead of continuing to ascend, the pleasure may impede us. We may come to a halt, remove our gear, and start examining the phenomena around us in an attempt to prolong the ecstatic feelings. Sometimes a butterfly will draw us off the path, luring us deep into the forest, exhausting us as we chase after its luminescent wings. Finally when it disappears, we will be lost in a dark wasteland. It may take a long time to find the trail again. One of the gorgeous butterflies that frequents the spiritual path is called "fantasy."

In this section of the book, we will explore pleasant mind states which are commonly experienced on retreat and some of the purer phenomena toward which all spiritual voyagers aspire, such as cosmic consciousness and union with the divine.

# FANTASY

Cartoon characters reveal their thoughts in balloons that float above their heads. When we read these thoughts, we are amused by things that we recognize in ourselves or have seen in others. While a cartoon character is in its thought bubble, it is having its own fantasy, but when the balloon pops open, *voilà!*—the character returns to cartoon reality. This may strike our funny bone because we too have experienced the shock of reentering a reality different from the one in which our minds tend to wander.

We live in a four-dimensional reality—the three dimensions of space and a fourth of time. The flatland of cartoons has only two dimensions—we must read from drawing to drawing and turn the page to simulate time. In so doing, we can bring our four-dimensional awareness into the cartoon reality and pretend that the fantasy figures are part of our reality of time and space, or we can see them for what they really are.

Most spiritual teachers acknowledge another dimension that transcends the four dimensions of time and space. This is the fifth dimension, the spiritual plane. A part of us always dwells in this timeless and spaceless realm. Each of us has this inner aspect—it is sometimes called our Observer, our Knower, or our Overseer. This

Overseer is not separate from us but is connected with our highest ephemeral aspect, which dwells in timeless realms, so the Overseer can leap into the future or the past. This teaching is difficult for our rational minds to appreciate because our perceptions are limited by the four dimensions. The mystic, however, is genuinely at home in the fifth dimension.

When the Overseer perceives that we are in the fantasy realm, it is something quite different from thought balloons hovering over our heads. That device works only in a flatland. In our spatial reality, we actually live *inside* the fantasy balloon—it encompasses us completely and is the only world we experience.

Most of us are fascinating characters for the Overseer. We are exceptionally creative as we invent world upon world in which to dwell. It does not matter that we may actually be in these worlds for only a few seconds. Indeed, if we did not wear watches we would have no idea of how much time we spent in this inner reality.

Although we cannot appreciate the fifth dimension logically, our imagination affords us entry into this magical realm. Once we understand that our imagination is our admission ticket to the Overseer's timeless world, where we can jump rapidly and effortlessly between past and future, we can engage our Overseer in a different level of conversation or even an entirely new fantasy. Now our power of imagination *really* becomes interesting. It is as though the cartoon characters could inflate themselves into three dimensions and jump into our lives to play with us.

Fantasy is a marvelous asset but can also be a devastating liability. It is a gateway not only into the angelic realms of the higher heavens but also the "hell realms" of demonic visions. In its less intense form, fantasy is with us throughout the day, sparking our hopes and fears, providing some of the driving force behind desire and aversion. In its more intense form, fantasy pulls us into universes where we are entirely out of contact with what is happening around us. These separate universes are continually changing, and many of us live in a constant dream state, whether our eyes are open or closed.

We are so accustomed to fantasy in our daily lives that we often do not realize how much our consciousness is dominated by it. Sitting quietly on retreat, we become aware of the awesome nature of this habit. The word *habit* is used because we have come to believe that this is the way our minds works. As our concentration practice develops, we realize that the mind works quite differently. Fantasy, when misused, greatly weakens the mind and keeps it from working efficiently and powerfully.

If we set ourselves the simple task of watching our breath, we find that very soon our minds start to wander and concentration is lost. Try it out. Close your eyes and put all your attention on the breath entering and leaving the body. Breathe normally. During the inhalation, try to have in your thoughts only the word *IN,* and during the exhalation only the word *OUT.* Keep just one other thought in mind: Count each round of IN and OUT. How many breaths can you count without thinking of anything other than the words IN or OUT?

Sounds simple, but most of us cannot count to ten without our minds drifting. Many of us cannot get to five. Hardly anyone but a master can consistently count to twenty with perfect concentration.

When we become more advanced as meditators, we are able to distinguish between the different elements of our thoughts. We discern that imagination may be sparked by a simple stimulus and developed through various associations. The mechanics of this process are complex and almost impossible to analyze. The syndrome can be interrupted, however, when the Overseer has an opportunity to view the fantasies and observe their patterns. This occurs when we slow down our activities and our mental processes, as naturally happens on retreat.

We have already discussed the dark side of fantasy in the section on demonic visions. Now we are considering the lighter side, particularly the seemingly harmless mental excursions we make as world travelers, romantic daredevils, heroic adventurers, clever comedians, irresistible conversationalists, wheeler-dealers, financial wizards, or any other pleasant fancy from the infinite resources of our fertile minds.

Some of us are inclined to dwell in light fantasies, while others have a propensity for the darker variety. Most people think that the light conjectures are fine but that something is wrong with anyone who frequents the dark realms. The latter may be true if someone becomes psychologically crippled through this association. However, an obsession with the lighter fantasies is just as spiritually devastating as an obsession with the dark variety.

One of the most corrupting fantasies we indulge in is that we are on our way to becoming somebody. Whoever that somebody is does not really matter. It is usually a great somebody, a successful somebody, a really loved somebody, or the best somebody in the world.

A key factor in the enlightenment process is our ability to subdue and ultimately vanquish the formidable barrier known as "becoming," this constant posture of leaning into the future, having expectations, projecting an ideal image of ourselves. It permeates our being and is always impinging on our consciousness. When we begin to see the patterns our fantasies form, we realize how much this sense of becoming dominates us. Even when we are moderately successful in bringing it into line, the idea of becoming something or somebody still lingers, waiting to hook us at our first sign of "progress."

Many of us have worked intensively to develop a quiet mind, only to have it shattered the moment we think: "Tranquillity! This is nice. I feel good. Now I'm getting somewhere. Soon I'll be enlightened." The actual experience of tranquillity vanishes at the first thought of recognition. *We cannot be tranquil and simultaneously think about it.* Thus our desire to become someone special is self-defeating, causing the frustrating experience of losing a marvelous experience whenever it appears.

Positive mind states are insidious because we do not clearly recognize what they are doing to us. We are seduced by them. They feel good to us. We have grown so accustomed to them that they become our self-image. Pleasant visions can produce an inflated image of ourselves, which in turn excites new fabrications to support it. This interrelationship builds a complex edifice that can supply a fiction about ourselves at the slightest provocation. After some time, the edifice becomes a mighty fortress which gives the impression that there is a self hidden somewhere inside. But it is really a facade like a Hollywood set, or the Wizard of Oz, who himself was really nobody but who could produce a marvelous fantasy to induce a false impression.

Time and again a retreatant engages in daydreams. One moment we are sitting quietly in concentration, the next we realize we are on the moon, getting ready to colonize a new solar system. Although we may discern what has happened, we are seduced because it feels good and we are curious to "see what happens." This habit of following a fantasy to its conclusion is part of the delusion that the dream somehow has a life of its own, or that a truth we need to know will be revealed.

It takes enormous discipline to let go of these notions. Some are easier to dissolve because we do not feel particularly attached to them. Others seem to be part of our lifeblood; they have an aura of importance or are so stimulating and exciting we can hardly imagine being without them. This is particularly true when we enter angelic realms and encounter wondrous beings filled with light and wisdom.

Such experiences tend to arise on intensive retreats. Most of them are pure fantasy, but some may be genuine transcendental experiences. It is important to note that fantasies have central qualities of willfulness and grasping—we reach for and hold on to images. In a transcendental experience, however, we have no volition or sense of ourselves. A simple test we can use when having a special experience during meditation is to ask where is the "I/me". The ability to pose the question is an indication of the presence of self-identity. In other words, if we still have a sense of self during an exceptional meditative experience, we can be assured it is simply an illusion. If there is no "I/me" thinking about what is happening and if the question never arises, we may be experiencing something extraordinary.

Whether or not we have transcended into new spiritual realms is a tricky issue. Most of us would like to experience a revelation and are easily deceived into be-lieving that we are on the road to enlightenment. This applies not only to fantasies but all kinds of enlightenment experiences. Without a qualified teacher, it is impossible for us to assess what has really happened.

The real question is: Why are we so drawn to hav-ing transcendental experiences? A major misconception among inexperienced meditators—and those experienced as well—is that the goal of spiritual work is the attainment of magical power. This is simply not the case.

A story is told about a fourth-century Christian monk who was part of the group known as the Desert Fathers:

> *To one of the brethren appeared a devil, transformed into an angel of light, who said to him: I am the Angel Gabriel, and I have been sent to thee. But the brother said: Think again—you must have been sent to somebody else. I haven't done anything to deserve an angel. Immediately the devil ceased to appear.*[1]

Most of our remarkable visions on retreat are generated in our imagination. There may be a slim chance that a particular experience is not simply imagination, but the most useful attitude we can have is to accept that it is nothing special, despite its allure. Titillating, yes. Essential, no. The skilled meditator moves on with the business at hand: one-pointed concentration, consistent effort, emptiness, and softness.

The attitude of "nothing special" is an excellent way to subdue excessive daydreaming. The best method to escape the fortress of self-delusion that we have built is to disassociate from every fantasy that arises. We must constantly remind ourselves that we can learn nothing from a fantasy; it has no substance. When we separate ourselves and do not feed these visions, they quickly vanish.

Every time we indulge in a fantasy, we prolong it, weakening our resolve and spoiling our concentration. Each time we allow one to linger, it exacts from us a price in clarity, firmness, and the will to push through to a new level. We must be merciless, using the sharp sword of discrimination to detach ourselves from these inventions.

It is difficult to do. Fantasies are often accompanied by highly pleasurable feelings. Yet, we must find a way to understand that this pleasure is only temporary. We can release the daydream and thereby strengthen our resolve, or we can indulge ourselves and weaken our concentration.

As with all thoughts that arise in the mind, we must not judge ourselves harshly. Thoughts come and go on their own. Fantasies will arise spontaneously. The tactic recommended for working with them, however, is more aggressive than the methods for working with negative thoughts like fear, aversion, pain, or doubt. In those situations, a simple observation of our internal process is sufficient to rid ourselves of these thoughts, as we have little desire to maintain a negative mind state. Fantasies, on the other hand, have a self-perpetuating quality and we need to be more forceful in distancing ourselves from them.

We either remind ourselves that it is "nothing special," of no consequence, or we can use another approach: the conscious introduction of visualization practices to redirect the fantasies from self-indulgence into higher realms. As we focus our imagination into spiritually nourishing arenas, we can counter the negative impact of fanciful daydreaming. Any visualization practice that is spiritually oriented will suffice. (See the chapter on visualization in my book, *Silence, Simplicity, and Solitude*.)

Working with fantasy becomes easier and at the same time more difficult as we go along. It is easier because through experience we recognize the insubstantiality of these mental voyages. They rapidly disappear when not given any attention. However, our work becomes increasingly difficult because when we are successful in inhibiting them, we enter a void. We have left behind the stimulation and pleasure of our daydreaming, but we have not yet achieved the harmony of a calm mind, which awaits us in future stages of meditation, such as tranquillity and equanimity. This void is perhaps the most difficult period during spiritual progress. Some call it "the long, dark night."

In the early stages of spiritual practice, a beginner often believes the most challenging aspect of the practice is dealing with negative mind states and demonic visions. As we become more experienced, however, we observe that it is far more difficult to give up the pleasurable mind states. This difficulty is magnified by the fact that rather than receive a reward when we distance ourselves from pleasurable experiences in our spiritual work, we face the prospect of a period of darkness.

When we speak of "giving up" pleasurable mind states, the beginning meditator might understand that it is necessary to avoid such experiences. This is not the intention. In our practice we will constantly encounter both pleasurable and unpleasurable experiences. We come to recognize that they appear on their own and will disappear. Just as we know naturally not to cling to our negative mind states, we are now learning the same approach to pleasurable thoughts that arise. We do not avoid the thought, nor do we cling to it. This is what is meant by "giving it up"; it is much easier said than done.

The only successful path as we let go of our desires and aversions is to sustain our faith as we continue our efforts. Some of us begin with this kind of faith, but most of us must develop it along the way as our practice strengthens and as we reflect upon the world around us. There are no prescriptions for acquiring such faith. A great paradox of the spiritual path is that strong faith is needed to persist in our quest, but we have no known method for securing it. Faith remains a mysterious but essential quality necessary for the spiritual journey.

# ECSTASY AND BLISS

In Kapleau's *The Three Pillars of Zen*, a middle-aged Japanese executive offers an account of his sudden illuminating experience after seven or eight years of being a meditator:

> *At midnight I abruptly awakened. At first my mind was foggy, then suddenly [the following] quotation flashed into my consciousness: "I came to realize clearly that Mind is no other than mountains, rivers, and the great wide earth, the sun and the moon and the stars." And I repeated it. Then all at once I was struck as though by lightning, and the next instant heaven and earth crumbled and disappeared. Instantaneously, like surging waves, a tremendous delight welled up in me, a veritable hurricane of delight, as I laughed loudly and wildly: "Ha, ha, ha, ha, ha, ha! There's no reasoning here, no reasoning at all! Ha, ha, ha!" The empty sky split in two, then opened its enormous mouth and began to laugh uproariously: "Ha, ha, ha!"*[2]

Ecstasy! Bliss! Joy! The supreme happiness of profound realization. Finally after all the effort, pain, doubt, and the long hours of tedium, many aspirants touch a new level of consciousness. Often it lasts for merely an instant, at times it remains for hours and even days. Many feel their lives are changed forever from the moment this new awareness appears.

Most meditators and retreatants who have given accounts of such experiences testify that it has taken many years to achieve a breakthrough, years marked by a discipline of regular meditation and regular periods of intensive practice on some form of retreat. Almost all turning-point experiences happen during or just following such practice. It is interesting that we use the word *intensive* rather than *extensive*. In the same way, it has been suggested that the word *ecstasy* when applied to the spiritual experience really would be more accurate if it were called *instasy*, because "the mystic is not carried out of himself but rather into the depths of himself, into 'the ocean of the soul,' as the poets might say."[3]

An oceanic experience has been described by mystics in all traditions and a common thread weaves through mystical narrative suggesting that all paths lead to the One. This would tend to refute the claim that any one path is superior to another. However, the language of mystics is often difficult to comprehend because the essential ideas cannot be articulated easily or communicated accurately to anyone who has not had a similar experience.

When we read the following description of a woman in the Zen Buddhist tradition relating her enlightenment breakthrough to two of her teachers, it sounds rather like a party:

> At dokusan [*a private interview with the teacher*] *I rushed into the little cottage my teacher was occupying and hugged and kissed him and shook Tai-san's hand, and let loose with such a torrent of comical verbosity that all three of us laughed with delight. The* roshi *tested and passed me, and I was officially ushered through the first barrier of the gateless gate.*[4]

When a spiritual teacher tests a student for a level of insight, it is not the kind of exam that has clear answers.

ECSTASY AND BLISS

The substance of a student's responses is not as significant as the quality of the student's behavior, which is what the teacher is able to see and hear.

There are many stories of enlightened men and women, often from widely divergent spiritual backgrounds, discovering a deep joy in each other's presence when they meet. One story tells of a well-known Sufi master who met a famous Zen monk for the first time. Each looked deeply into the other's eyes. They never said hello or shook hands. They just stared into each other's soul for over an hour. Finally, each bowed to the other and asked to be his disciple.

As our awareness expands, we change; we not only become different, we notice new things in others. Most retreatants, even in the early stages of development, encounter periods of rapture, ecstasy, or bliss. At the time, it feels like the most profound experience of our lives; all the earlier struggle is washed away, and the entire process seems worthwhile. But, once again, we are in danger if we believe we have reached the goal of our spiritual work.

Ecstasy and bliss are among the most dangerous aspects of the enlightenment process. Who would choose pain over bliss, or boredom over ecstasy? The experience of joy is one of the most sensual highs known to humankind. It is so seductive, people have been known to give up family, friends, business, and all else in the pursuit of such experience. However, ecstasy experience has also derailed people from spiritual paths by leading them into a cul-de-sac called the "taste of bliss."

It is difficult for us to realize that pleasure also can be an enemy. This is especially true when most of the effort in the process of spiritual purification is demanding, difficult, and often painful. This barrier to spiritual growth

PLEASANT MIND STATES

is actually a double-edged sword. Pleasure lures us away from the awakening process; the effort to maintain or repeat it agitates the mind so that we are grasping for things rather than letting go.

The taste of great pleasure, which is positive, will often arouse the negative state of desire. Ramana Maharshi said:

> The final obstacle in meditation is ecstasy; you feel great bliss and happiness and want to stay in that ecstasy. Do not yield to it but pass on to the next stage which is great calm. The calm is higher than ecstasy and it merges into samādhi.[5]

I remember sitting in a long retreat, having just observed another moment of bliss fade away. I felt a rush of self-pity that "they" would not let me maintain even this tiny pleasure, which surely I deserved after all those days of severe discipline. For me, letting go of pleasure is always the most challenging test.

The closer we come to our spiritual objective, the more difficult the endeavor. People often believe the aim of spiritual work is bliss, ecstasy, or joy. Indeed, many of the accounts we read describe these states. A number of modern Western "enlightenment" programs and seminars promise these experiences as the end point of their practice. They can probably guarantee them since it is not difficult to induce periods of bliss or ecstasy with robust meditation practices, such as mantra, visualization, and breathing techniques.

The meditator, however, will soon realize that bliss is a passing phenomenon. It was fun while it lasted, but now what do we do? This is exactly the point made by most teachers. Having fun is not the purpose of spiritual practice, and thus they teach us to treat ecstasy in exactly the same way as we cope with pain during our meditation practice. We observe it as it arises, perceive its true nature, and watch it fade away into oblivion.

Shivapuri Baba also teaches caution:

> *The bliss you experience in your moments of God-worship should not be cared for. If you know this bliss you meditate on the bliss and not on God. Therefore ignore this bliss and think only of God.*[6]

When I started on this path, nobody told me I was going to have to ignore my bliss! There is precious little of it, and I thought it would be something I would gather carefully, like gold nuggets in a stream. In fact, some of my earlier retreats were filled with elation and I thought I was getting close to enlightenment because it felt so good. The truth of the matter came when I realized that periods of elation were always followed by periods filled with drudgery. I had no way to predict my moods from one retreat to the next, from day to day, or even from hour to hour.

Our pleasurable experiences come in degrees, beginning with mild elation, increasing in intensity until reaching the highest peaks of ecstasy. Each stage has new powers of seduction that pull us away from the path. This becomes most apparent when we have practiced sufficiently to observe intensely blissful or ecstatic states. Just when we believe our thoughts are under control, a new pleasure level blossoms. As long as we are firmly in the observer mode, the meditation flows smoothly. All too often, however, we are startled by the "Aha!" level.

"Aha!" can be said only from an awareness of "I/me." The realization of "I am in bliss," or "I am in ecstasy," is sufficient to ruin everything. An enormous gap separates the experience of being in ecstasy without any sense of ourselves and that of recognizing we are in ecstasy. The authentic accounts of meditative bliss and ecstasy are after the fact. As soon as a person identifies with a pleasurable mind state, as soon as "I" have a sense of myself as the one experiencing, the meditative state becomes constricted and bounded by the ego. This is why these pleasurable experiences are a major barrier to the higher levels of consciousness. We tend to hold on to them and they constantly pull us back into ourselves.

Once we are adequately warned, it becomes a matter of practice to develop the skills and discipline to approach ecstatic experiences just like any other. Over time, we will find that they come and go and are nothing special. When we relinquish our desire for ecstasy and bliss, we will have access to the realms of love, tranquillity, equanimity, divine inspiration, union with the divine, and complete awareness.

These higher realms also come to us and fade away, but they have a different quality from the basic pleasurable mind states of bliss, ecstasy, and joy. The basic states nourish us and provide sustenance for our ongoing effort; however, as we shall see, these higher levels of meditative experience permeate us so thoroughly, we are transformed. Once again, we must not idealize these, or desire to have them; they will come when we are ready—they are the natural fruit of our spiritual labors.

# LOVE

*The voice of my beloved! Behold, he comes leaping upon the mountains, skipping upon the hills. My beloved is like a gazelle or a young hart; behold, he stands behind our wall, he looks in at the windows; he peers through the lattice. My beloved spoke, and said to me, Rise up, my love, my fair one, and come away. For, lo, the winter is past, the rain is over and gone; the flowers appear on the earth; the time of the singing bird is come, and the voice of the turtledove is heard in our land; the fig tree puts forth her green figs, and the vines in blossom give their scent. Arise, my love, my fair one, and come away.*[7]

The Song of Songs is a deeply mystical expression that confuses many readers by its sensual metaphors. It employs the theme of love to explore the essence of relationship, in this instance between the Creator and creation. This motif of love pervades Western spiritual literature. A contemporary reader might blush at the imagery used by medieval monks and nuns. The *Zohar*, the principal source book of Kabbalah, is replete with sexual metaphors. The Sufis are extravagant and rapturous in their love poems.

One of the most famous works in Christian mysticism, *The Spiritual Canticle* of St. John of the Cross, is filled with such images:

PLEASANT MIND STATES

*My Beloved, the mountains, the solitary wooded valleys; the strange islands, the sonorous rivers, the whisper of the amorous breezes; the tranquil night. At the time of the rising of the dawn, the silent music, the sounding solitude, the supper that recreates and enkindles love. Our flowery bed, encompassed with dens of lions, hung with purple and builded in peace. Crowned with a thousand shields of gold. In the track of thy footprint the young girls run along by the way. At the touch of a spark, at the spiced wine, flows forth the Divine balsam. In the inner cellar of my Beloved have I drunk. And, when I went forth over all this meadow, then knew I naught and lost the flock which I followed aforetime. There he gave me his breast. There he taught me a science most delectable. And I gave myself to him indeed, reserving nothing. There I promised him to be his bride.*[8]

We tend to confuse such descriptions of the relationship between the Divine and creation with more common popular literature that expresses the relationship between human beings. Although there are always parallels between the spiritual and material worlds—the divine spark permeates all existence—mystics indicate that love on the spiritual planes far transcends anything we could possibly experience with each other.

It is difficult for us to understand what a nun means when she says she is married to Christ. Many of us cannot imagine how spiritual devotees, whether Buddhist, Hindu, or Christian, accept the discipline of celibacy. Thousands of descriptions testify that the experiences of these mystics far exceed the rewards of earthly love. Judaism and Islam have little precedent for celibacy, and the family is a primary aspect of each tradition, but strong emphasis is still placed on the love of God as prevailing over all earthly love.

During a retreat it is not uncommon to feel great waves

of love. This can be overwhelming when we reflect upon people we know well. At other times, the feelings are more diffuse; they radiate outward to include casual acquaintances or beyond to the world in general. We may have loving feelings toward all peoples, animals, plants, the smallest ant, and the largest redwood. At these moments our cheeks glow, we are filled with a new dimension of love, a sense of universality.

This overpowering experience comes and goes just like all other phenomena, but it has an afterglow which some teachers assert is the result of dwelling, even momentarily, in our natural, true condition. Our daily experience of separation and alienation is not our original state, but an illusion. The openness that results from the feeling of universal love is our birthright, and thus each time we enter it we are able to release some of the limiting thoughts that maintain our illusion of separation.

The residual effect of these loving experiences builds strength over a period. Frequently we will not notice the change taking place because the effort of maintaining our concentration keeps us locked in a personal universe. When a retreat comes to an end, however, our loving feelings pour out. The culmination of a group retreat of ten days or longer is almost always marked by the radiance of a genuine opening of heart and soul. People who do not know each other and who did not exchange a word may communicate deep compassion and tenderness toward each other the first time they converse.

There is a distinct difference between these loving feelings and fantasies that lead to romantic illusions. With a fantasy, we always have a sense of ourselves. Yet, when we feel true, expansive love, all the edges of our self-identity are blurred, and we gain a new understanding of shared experience and universality. This level of love is not associated with desire or sexuality because it does not have its source in the individual ego.

Ego-oriented love has an inherent duality—the lover and the beloved. Universal love is described by mystics as lover, beloved, and the essence of love all being one—it is egoless. The source of this love is the Divine.

Rav Abraham Isaac Kook speaks of this:

> Love in its most luminous aspect has its being beyond the world, in the divine realm, where there are no contradictions, limits, or opposition; only bliss and good, wide horizons without limit. When worldly love derives from it, it partakes in much of its nature. . . . When these love-possessed people see the world, especially living creatures full of quarrels, hatred, persecutions, and conflicts, they yearn with all their being to share in those aspirations that move life toward comprehensiveness and unity, peace and tranquillity. They feel and they know that the nearness of God, for which they yearn, can only lead them to joining themselves with all for the sake of all.[9]

This is the true transcendental love, yearning to join with everything rather than to have something for oneself. Pierre Teilhard de Chardin, the eminent twentieth-century Jesuit theologian and philosopher, suggests this "super-love" is a necessity if we wish to extract ourselves from the limitations and alienation that rules our separateness. He says the only way to achieve unanimity is to have a convergence at the center, which is the ultimate Ego at the summit of the universe. Without this oneness, our individual egos will always keep us in a state of separation.[10]

As long as these ideas remain philosophical, until we feel a spark of this universal love in our own hearts, the concept of universal love remains an abstraction and consequently does not have real power. This is a significant reason retreatants persist. Our sustained efforts in an intensive retreat almost always initiate strong loving feelings. Of course, few will leave a retreat with a heart full of universal love. Each of us has a wide array of defense mechanisms that continue to harden us in feelings of separateness despite deep meditation, but as we become more advanced in the enlightenment process, we remove the barriers that separate us from the rest of the world and thus are more able to express this love.

At the highest levels of awareness, the feelings of universal love can reach awesome proportions. Gershom Scholem teaches us:

> In its sublimest manifestations, pure fear of God is identical with love and devotion for Him, not from a need for protection against the demons, or from a fear of temptation, but because in this mystical state a flood of joy enters the soul and sweeps away every trace of mundane and egotistical feeling.[11]

Scholem goes on to quote a well-known Jewish mystic, Rabbi Eleazar of Worms:

> The soul is full of love of God and bound with ropes of love, in joy and lightness of heart. . . . For when the soul thinks deeply about the fear of God, then the flame of heartfelt love bursts in it and the exultation of innermost joy fills the heart. . . . And the lover thinks not of his advantage in the world, he does not care about the pleasures of his wife or of his sons and daughters, but all this is as nothing to him . . . except that he may do the will of his Creator, do good unto others, keep sanctified the name of God. . . . And all the contemplation of his thought burns in the fire of love for Him.[12]

The Sufis have many examples of utter surrender in this state of mind. A famous Sufi mystic of the eighth century was a woman named Rabia, a freed slave girl. It is said:

> Rabia's love of God was absolute; there was no room left for any other thought or love. She did not marry, nor did she give the

*Prophet [Muhammad] a special place in her piety. The world meant nothing to her. She would shut the windows in spring without looking at the flowers and become lost in the contemplation of Him who created flowers and springtime. . . .*[13]

At first it is difficult to accept that we could find more beauty within a darkened room in contemplation of the Creator than in the presence of the creation. If we had the choice, however, of being in an empty room with our loved one or being forever alone in a room filled with gold and jewels, which would we choose? For Rabia, the world would be a lonely treasure without the prospect of absolute love.

A well-known poem composed by Rumi offers insight into the true nature of love. The poem describes a man constantly calling to and praising Allah. The Devil appears and asks the man how he can continue to call on God without ever getting the response "Here I am." As a result of this taunt, the man becomes broken-hearted and stops calling to Allah. One day he sees in a dream Khidr, the guide of mystics, who asks him why he has stopped calling to God. He answers that God never responded to his call and thus fears that he is being turned away from the door. Khidr replies, "That 'Allah' of yours *is* the 'Here I am.' "[14]

The calling out *is* the response. The question *is* the answer. It is all one. We do not just express love for the Divine; the Divine is the actual source of this expression. This is a typical Sufi conundrum where love is constantly flowing out and back to its source. The great mystics do not feel as though they are loving something. They do not exist separately from the beloved; love is simply pouring from the divine source. The awareness of being a vehicle for this continuous expression is the most profound experience we can have of the universal nature of pure love.

In the beginning, we are simply able to dip a toe into the boundless pool of love. When we do so, a soft warmth radiates through our bodies, and if we could, we would jump right in. But it is not so accessible. It takes continuing effort to detach ourselves from our own illusions and sense of limitations. This is what the practice is about. On some retreats we are able to feel close to this divine source, and part of our bodies become immersed in the luxurious waters of love; on others we can see the pool only from a distance.

As time goes on we soften, we open, and our potential for loving increases. This happens despite the hardships of spiritual effort and the ongoing predicament of our lives. The knowledge of the continuing process pulls us, encouraging more growth, and we constantly progress on the infinite path of expanding consciousness.

# CALMNESS AND TRANQUILLITY

People who are not experienced in meditation associate it with calmness or tranquillity. Meditation is frequently viewed as a kind of medicine to cure the effects of our constant activity and the nervousness of everyday life. Many do use meditation in this way, just as many practitioners of yoga use yogic practice for exercise or weight control. However, when the primary orientation of our practice is focused on physical or mental needs, the spiritual benefits are minimized.

The simple act of stopping all our activities and sitting silently, preferably in a quiet room, is usually sufficient to bring a sense of calmness. In the beginning stages of the practice everyone who meditates experiences this kind of calmness, the initial release of the stress and tension of normal daily engagement. As the practice develops, and especially during retreats, there is a new level of calmness which results in deep stillness and tranquillity that permeates everything happening in the moment.

Tranquillity is not ordinary relaxation. It is a state of mind that is the basis for new insights. A well-known metaphor for this is a pond of muddy water whose inner currents are constantly stirring up the mud so that all we can see is the pond's surface. Once the inner currents are quiet, the mud will settle and we can see into the depths. Confucius said:

> Men do not mirror themselves in running water—they mirror themselves in still water. Only what is still can still the stillness of other things.[15]

The first level of calmness is the experience of stilling the waters. When the material in the water settles down, then comes the more profound experience, which is often accompanied by an extraordinary sense of well-being, especially for those who experience it for the first time in their lives. Most of us are accustomed to being constantly agitated and we cannot imagine life any other way. Some people are so amazed by this initial experience of deep tranquillity that they may feel they have suddenly become enlightened.

The experienced retreatant recognizes that this state comes and goes. The more we sit, the more often it appears. As the practice becomes more integrated in our lives, our periods of tranquillity become more penetrating. They evolve from momentary and transient experiences to familiar companions. When that happens, tranquillity becomes the springboard for new levels of awareness.

The Jewish mystics believe that the state of divine inspiration called prophecy was dependent upon attaining a high level of tranquillity. Aryeh Kaplan notes:

> The most influential classical Judaic philosophers and Kabbalists clearly stated that meditation was the most important of all disciplines required to attain enlightenment and prophecy. Sources dating from Talmudic times teach that prophecy involves a high degree of mental quietude. Jeremiah's disciple, Baruch ben Neriah [who was not successful in attaining prophecy] said, "I have not

PLEASANT MIND STATES

*found serenity." An ancient Midrash comments, "Serenity is nothing other than prophecy." The spiritual power and enlighten-ment that is the most important element of the prophetic experience is not found in the whirlwind or earthquake, but in the "still small voice" of utter tranquillity. This is a state that is attained through deep meditation.[16]*

Many of us would settle for a little tranquillity in our lives. The aspirant knows that it is but a stepping stone to more advanced stages, which is vital to realize, for tranquillity also can lure people from the path of enlighten-ment. In Buddhism it is sometimes called the "cave of Satan" or the "pit of pseudo-emancipation." It is a "stage in *zazen* where one experiences absolute serenity and is bedeviled into believing it to be self-realization. It requires an inspired effort to break out and go beyond this state."[17]

In our practice we are constantly challenged by the dilemma that it is almost impossible for us to experience intensely pleasurable states without strengthening the notion of "I/me" in the process. As long as this continues to happen, we remain deluded and our path is blocked by a huge wall of personal identification. While we cling to pleasure, we not only lose the ability to transcend it, but the pleasure itself soon disappears, following the inexo-rable law that "all things must pass."

At times, a meditator will enter into a feeling of nothingness that may be confused with tranquillity. This self-induced trance is like an empty dream in which we feel neither good nor bad. Indeed, we feel nothing because nothing is happening.

Tranquillity can be distinguished from this meditative catatonia. The tranquil frame of mind maintains a pres-ence of continuous awareness. Although our reactions may be tempered when we are deeply calm, our senses are not barricaded, we continue to experience incoming stimuli. However, when we are in a frozen mind state, we miss most things because our sensory apparatus is shut down.

True tranquillity is a state of clear perception. Ramana Maharshi said, "The tranquil clarity, which is devoid of mental turmoil, alone is the *samādhi* which is the firm base for liberation. By earnestly trying to destroy the deceptive mental turmoil, [we will] experience that *samādhi* as the peaceful consciousness which is inner clarity."[18] There is no sleepiness in the tranquil state: It assures sharpness and clarity.

This "base for liberation" opens to a number of higher paths. It is as though we have set up a base camp halfway up the mountain of enlightenment, and now there are a number of alternative routes to make an assault on the supreme peak. One of these paths is called equanimity, another is known as divine inspiration, and a third is named union with the Divine. The mountain peak is not an end point where we can plant a flag, but a singular place where we step out of this dimension of time and space into an entirely new universe. Although this summit of transition has many names, we will call it cosmic consciousness.

I have had only brief encounters with these states of being. Therefore, much of the following is not written from experience, but with the faith that has come out of fleeting but extraordinary episodes. We now begin an expedition into an immense territory that extends beyond any universe known to astronomers. There are no boundaries here, and we must enter with the deepest humility.

Many masters will not discuss these states of being. They maintain that descriptions are impossible and moreover could be detrimental because they excite false expectations or encourage a corrupting desire. We must balance against this risk, however, the fact that some people experience high levels of consciousness without a teacher, and these episodes can be overwhelming and disorienting. It has been comforting for me to read about other people's experiences to gain perspective. Familiarity with these testimonies adds strength of purpose in the difficult early stages of practice, and it helps us recognize an authentic state.

Let us now take a gentle excursion to the highest levels of meditative and retreat experience, keeping in mind that words are inadequate to describe these states fully. If we allow the ideas to sink into our intuitive being, and then into the deeper levels of the soul, we will recognize the truth.

# EQUANIMITY AND PEACE

Equanimity is sometimes equated incorrectly with calmness and tranquillity, but it is a different attribute. The experience of calmness or tranquillity has a sensual quality of pleasure that often makes us aware of ourselves and sometimes excites a desire to maintain this pleasant state of mind. Equanimity, on the other hand, arises from true insight into the constant changing nature of creation. When we deeply realize this truth, desire evaporates and aversion disappears. Until we have reached this understanding, we continue to rationalize our desires. We may say, "Yes, I am aware that all things change, but companionship, wealth, or happiness is surely preferable to loneliness, poverty, or sadness." Someone who has attained equanimity could not make this statement, for there are no preferences to cloud the understanding that everything is impermanent.

At first this may sound somewhat dry—an experiential state devoid of emotions, but nothing could be further from the truth. In a state of equanimity all the emotions that arise are felt, and attraction or rejection is experienced in its most elemental form. However, there will be no conditioned response to the stimuli. The feeling is there, but the reaction is not the usual one.

When we suffer from physical pain, we automatically

seek relief. Even when we believe we are sitting quietly, a close examination of our mental processes will usually uncover our subtle efforts to avert pain in some way. Someone who has attained equanimity does not react to pain. A good example of this is the story related earlier about Rabbi Akiva, who calmly recited his prayers as he was slowly flayed to death.

Such a person is clearly indifferent to personal attainment, goals, desires, and even the most basic sense of survival. History has proven there are some values more powerful than the survival instinct, and the pull toward enlightenment is one of these. In a state of equanimity we transcend the survival instinct since it is based on a sense of self-identity that no longer exists.

Although such indifference is related to aspects that we identify with "I/me," values that are not related to the self may be strongly experienced. For example, the person with equanimity has enormous compassion for the suffering in the world. Most of our suffering comes from our desires and aversions; it results in frustration and heartache—it is the human predicament. Thus the *bodhisattva,* one who has attained perfect equanimity and who dedicates all of his or her efforts to relieving suffering, is a paradigm of compassion.

At first it appears to be a contradiction of terms for someone to be indifferent to their own survival but at the same time filled with compassion. Yet, the inconsistency remains only as long as we have the idea that compassion is a personality trait. Once we recognize that it is a universal truth upon which the creation is built, the contradiction disappears.

In the Kabbalah, the divine source, called the *Ain Sof* (the Limitless) is viewed as the Great Bestower. Since it is infinite, encompassing everything, nothing exists outside of it and thus it cannot receive—it can only give. The cosmology of creation in Kabbalah suggests a continuous imperative—or "will"—for the *Ain Sof* to give because giving is one of its essential attributes. We noted in the chapter on purification that since the *Ain Sof* is infinite, nothing outside of it exists to receive, and thus it must somehow manifest a "will to receive."[19] The cosmology of how this occurs is complex and has far-reaching implications, but the key for us to understand is the principle that God gives and the creation receives. This divine "giving" stems from the qualities of mercy, which include wisdom, goodness, and compassion.

Many theologians believe that the most amazing gift of the human race is that we have the potential to imitate our Creator. On this matter, Moses Cordovero, a famous sixteenth-century Jewish mystic of the city of Safed not far from Jerusalem, wrote: "It is proper for man to imitate his Creator, resembling Him in both likeness and image according to the secret of the Supernal Form [the highest potential of human beings]."[20] Cordovero goes on to describe how we can imitate the Creator through thirteen attributes, including wisdom and compassion. The process of imitating divine qualities is a primary path for enlightenment.

When a person attains equanimity and thereby loses all self-interest, he or she transcends, so to speak, an aspect of the "will to receive." The person's physical existence requires this "will to receive" in its most primordial form, which is the binding force of all matter in creation, but in the higher realms of the mind, the person attains complete selflessness. This is expressed through selfless giving, which is the most essential attribute of the *tzaddik* in Judaism, the saint in Christianity, Islam, and Hinduism, and the *bodhisattva* in

Buddhism. Father Thomas Keating discusses this quality from a Christian perspective:

> *This disposition of giving everything away—one's time, energy, space, virtues, spirituality, and finally oneself—is not really giving anything away because, in the truest sense, whatever we give away, we are giving to ourselves. The gesture of opening one's hand is the same gesture as receiving.*
>
> *This emptying of ourselves for the good of others is a continuation of the same movement of emptying—kenosis—that goes on in the Trinity: giving away (or throwing away) all that the Father is to the Son and vice-versa, and each receiving everything back in and through the Person of infinite love, the Holy Spirit. As one manifests this love, one is giving everything away and receiving everything in return again and again, but each time with greater inclusiveness. The same love that one gives away keeps coming back. . . . This compassionate, nonjudgmental, selfless love is the Source of all that is; the ultimate beatitude is to disappear into it.*[21]

In Buddhism, the enlightened, generous state of mind is referred to as *bodhicitta*. It does not have a simple definition, but is recognized as a nucleus of human awareness—or the Buddha mind. A Tibetan lama, Chobgye Thicchen Rimpoche, commented that *bodhicitta* centers on love and compassion. Thomas Merton records that Thicchen spoke of three kinds of *bodhicitta*:

> 1) *"kingly"—in which one seeks spiritual power to save oneself and then save others;*
> 2) *"that of boatman"—in which one ferries oneself together with others to salvation;*
> 3) *"that of shepherd"—in which one goes behind all the others and enters salvation last—and this is the most perfect.*[22]

At another point, Merton describes *bodhicitta* as being comprised of two main factors: *sūnyatā,* the level of enlightenment that recognizes no substance, no essence that is real; and *karunā,* universal compassion.[23] The interfacing of *sūnyatā* and *karunā* is the fundamental principle of all who enter the world of the *bodhisattva.* Thus, a primary component of the state of equanimity is the unlimited expression of compassion, without any attachment and beyond all self-interest.

Another notable characteristic of equanimity is its all-encompassing peace—a sense of being "at one" with the universe. This is called by William James the "state of assurance." He notes that direct experience is essential for understanding this peace, which he describes as

> the . . . *sense that all is ultimately well with one, the peace, the harmony, the* willingness to be, *even though the outer conditions* [*of our situation*] *should remain the same. The certainty of God's grace, of justification, salvation, is an objective belief that usually accompanies the change* [*from ordinary feeling to harmonious peacefulness*] *in Christians; but this* [*faith in God*] *may be entirely lacking and yet the affective peace remain the same.*[24]

The key phrase, which James himself italicizes, is *will-ingness to be.* This "letting go" is the product of equanimity, which in the vernacular is called "going with the flow." When we are able to accomplish this release without the slightest resistance, a great peace pervades. James points out that this produces two additional benefits: an entirely new perception of the deeper truths of creation and an extraordinary freshness in every object perceived.[25] This is a major stage in the enlightenment process.

When we become aware that matter itself is not substantial, a shift takes place and everything assumes a new glow, as if it were disappearing and reappearing each moment. A typical account of transformation was re-corded a couple hundred years ago by Christian theolo-gian Jonathan Edwards:

*After this [enlightenment experience] my sense of divine things gradually increased and became more and more lively, and had more of that inward sweetness. The appearance of everything was altered; there seemed to be, as it were, a calm, sweet cast, or appearance of divine glory, in almost everything. God's excellency, his wisdom, his purity and love, seemed to appear in everything; in the sun, moon, and stars; in the clouds and blue sky; in the grass, flowers, and trees; in the water and all nature. . . . And scarce anything, among all the works of nature, was so sweet to me as thunder and lightning; formerly nothing had been so terrible to me. Before, I used to be uncommonly terrified with thunder, and to be struck with terror when I saw a thunderstorm rising; but now, on the contrary, it rejoices me.*[26]

It is important to understand that the peace associated with equanimity does not stem from confidence in the existence of objects, or even the universe itself; it is rather a pure recognition that things are not at all as they seem. The creation is constantly in flux. Although we normally associate peace with a sense of security, this peace arises from the realization that insecurity is a universal truth. As long as we seek to know something or to gain enlightenment, our goal will remain elusive. When we clearly understand that the infinite is by definition unknowable, its nature unattainable, and we integrate this fact with our deepest awareness of impermanence, the birth and death cycle that permeates all creation, we gain true equanimity and its companion of peace.

Ramana Maharshi speaks of this:

*Peace is your natural state. It is the mind that obstructs the natural state. Your* vichara *[self-inquiry] has been made only in the mind. Investigate what the mind is, and it will disappear. There is no such thing as mind apart from thought. Nevertheless, because of the emergence of thought, you surmise something from which it starts and term that the mind. When you probe to see what it is, you find there is really no such thing as mind. When the mind has thus vanished, you realize eternal peace.*[27]

There is yet another method to experience this peace, which was suggested by the anonymous fourteenth-century author of *The Cloud of Unknowing*. This writer emphasizes the idea of nothingness:

*I will speak in paradoxes. Do not try to withdraw into yourself [to live the interior life], for to put it simply, I do not want you to be anywhere; no, not outside, above, behind, or beside your-self. . . . I would indeed have you be nowhere. Why? Because nowhere, physically, is everywhere spiritually.*

*When your mind consciously focuses on anything, you are there in that place spiritually, as certainly as your body is located in a definite place right now. . . . Don't worry if your faculties fail to grasp it [nothingness]. Actually, that is the way it should be, for this nothingness is so lofty that they cannot reach it. It cannot be explained, only experienced. [At first] it will feel very dark and inscrutable indeed. But truly, they are blinded by the splendor of its spiritual light. . . . For in this darkness we experience an intuitive understanding of everything material and spiritual without giving special attention to anything in particular.*[28]

Nothingness is another facet of equanimity. In essence, this writer is speaking of no desire, aversion, space, or personal identity. Giving up self-identity, moderating passions, and the intense effort to break lifelong patterns are all frightening prospects. Sometimes a glimpse into the emptiness of the unconditioned mind can cause us to bolt back into the comfort of the busy, confused mind which has been our home for so long. Even after a great deal of work, many people turn back when they arrive at one of the higher gates of enlightenment.

The true adventurer is courageous enough to proceed. Standing in emptiness, without attachment or identification, is like the initial vertical drop on a roller coaster. We leave part of ourselves behind and descend in a screeching free-fall. Then: the abyss. This roller coaster never goes into its first turn. It just falls and falls until we do not feel as though we are falling anymore. We enter a state where there is no gravity. Nothing pulls at us. In the beginning this may be terrifying but after a while, we realize there will be no crash. There is nothing more to fear. With this realization a deep peace suffuses everything.

Then we may recognize in those around us the fear of collision that prevents them from letting go. We see how they cling to material things—things that are certain to slip away. We may try to share the knowledge that there is nothing to fear and that all the grasping is futile. Sometimes they hear, and sometimes they do not hear. Our experience nonetheless remains profoundly peaceful, exceedingly clear.

The peace derived through equanimity transcends the pleasurable states of bliss, ecstasy, or tranquillity. It is deeper, more difficult to attain, and longer lasting. The realization of authentic equanimity is transformative. It is not a potential cul-de-sac like many other states because by definition it is without desire or aversion. Indeed, it is one of the highest levels of consciousness we can realize.

Throughout our years of practice we will certainly experience periods of equanimity. These periods come and go. Masters teach, however, that when we achieve the highest levels of discipline, we may enter a permanent state of peace and clarity. Even without this assurance, when we experience true peace for even the briefest moments, we gain a profound affirmation in the potential of our existence. This alone is sufficient to encourage our steady practice in the ongoing quest for deeper under-standing.

# DIVINE INSPIRATION

The monotheistic traditions all acknowledge a divine Creator and agree that the source of creation is unknowable. The infinite cannot be perceived by the finite. There may be impressions, hints, or clues, but certain knowledge is unattainable.

In addition to this theological view, the mystical position is that the Creator *must* remain hidden for any possibility of free will. If we could prove the existence of a Creator, if we could catch the slightest glimpse, the awesome nature of this truth would be so compelling there would no longer be any opportunity for free choice. Therefore, not only is the infinite unknowable, but of necessity it is concealed from the finite.

Yet, the theological perspective suggests there is a way to know the Creator—the key ingredient is faith. According to this view, when faith is predominant in our search for truth, we have the capacity to experience divine inspiration. This is a remarkable paradox of religious teaching. God cannot be known to anyone who doubts, but will be revealed to the individual who believes.

In our Age of Reason we reject this idea as a self-fulfilling delusion. It has been observed that if a person believes anything strongly enough, he or she will find ways to make it seem true. Of course, the same argument may be used to defend religious faith. Theologians suggest that those who believe the reasoning mind is "almighty" have a strong conviction that reason will ultimately reveal Truth. This conviction is so robust, rationalists cannot accept the possibility of any truth as ultimately unprovable. Thus, in the opinion of the theologians, the belief that all truth is verifiable is also a delusion. This difference of opinion is the cornerstone of the ongoing battle between faith and reason.

Mystics believe the debate between faith and reason is necessary and will never be resolved. Each time there is an attempt to synthesize faith and reason another chasm will separate them. Reason is the foundation of a universe that operates with time and space while faith is the foundation of the timeless, spiritual dimension. One cannot exist without the other and there must always be a tension between them.

An eminent eighteenth-century Kabbalist, Moses Hayim Luzzatto, known as the Ramhal, discusses this point in his famous work *Derech HaShem* (The Way of God):

> God ordained that man should naturally be able to teach himself, understand and reason with his intellect, and thus gain knowledge from his observation of things and their properties. On the basis of this, man is also able to infer and deduce things that are not immediately apparent, and can thus gain a more complete understanding of things. This is the natural process of human reason.
>
> God also decreed, however, that there exist another means of gaining knowledge that is much higher than this. This is what we call bestowed enlightenment.
>
> Bestowed enlightenment consists of an influence granted by God through various particular means especially prepared for this purpose. When this influence reaches an individual's mind, certain information becomes fixed in it. He perceives this knowledge clearly, without any doubt or error, and knows it completely,

*with all its propositions and corollaries, as well as its place in the*
*general scheme. This is called Divine Inspiration* [Ruah Ha-
kodesh].[29]

There are actually three levels of divine inspiration.
The lowest level is the unseen hand that guides the words
and actions of a person. Although someone must be
worthy of this gift in order to receive it, it is granted
without the person's knowledge. At the next level, a
person is aware that God is guiding his or her speech and
actions. There are many degrees of this kind of divine
inspiration, from automatic writing and guidance of an
inner voice to actually consulting oracles. The highest
level of divine inspiration is called prophecy, which
comes through trances and visions.[30]

The Jewish perspective is that the kind of prophecy
recorded in the Bible was originally available to all
humankind but is not currently accessible. The reason for
this is that an indispensable condition for prophecy is joy,
according to Jewish sages. Obviously, the world these
days is not a particularly happy place. Anger, depression,
sadness, hostility, and other self-destructive acts diminish
the possibility for prophetic visions. The current mood of
the world precludes the highest level of "bestowed
enlightenment." Still, the belief endures that the future
holds a renewal of this level of joy and prophecy will be
reestablished.

A prominent thirteenth-century Jewish mystic, Abraham Abulafia, claimed to have experienced true prophecy. This was highly controversial because he lived in
Europe and it was believed by medieval Jewish scholars
that prophecy could be realized only in the Holy Land.
Aryeh Kaplan writes: "Abulafia refused to accept this
literally, and said that the Holy Land discussed in this
teaching referred to a specific spiritual level. If an indi-

PLEASANT MIND STATES

vidual reached this level, he could attain prophecy, no matter what his geographical location."[31] This is a position typical of mysticism, which always seeks to broaden literal interpretations.

Just as the Jewish tradition asserts that biblical prophecy is not part of our contemporary enlightenment process, Muslims believe Muhammad was the last of the prophets. Nonetheless, for hundreds of years, Sufis have worked with various levels of divine inspiration just as Abulafia did. In fact, they employed some of the same methods. Abulafia meditated on Hebrew letters and mentally performed permutations of these letters until he attained a level of inspiration. We find also that "some of the prayers practiced by certain Sufis, mainly in later periods, are in fact very close to magical incantation: the master played with the letters of the Arabic alphabet, he composed prayers by deriving every possible word from a particular Arabic root, for example the root underlying a specific divine name, or wrote prayers in alphabetical order, filling them with certain words and letters that are considered powerful and impressive."[32]

Sufi poetry is often divinely inspired. Many of the poems are love songs, while some try to communicate ineffable mysteries. In the tenth century Ibn Ata wrote:

> *When men of common parlance question us, we answer them with signs mysterious and dark enigmas; for the tongue of man cannot express so high a truth, whose span surpasses human measure. But my heart has known it, and has known of it a rapture that thrilled and filled my body, every part. Seest thou not, these mystic feelings capture the very art of speech, as men who know vanquish and silence their unlettered foe.*[33]

Teresa of Avila teaches us:

> *[When] . . . the spirit truly seems to go forth from the body . . . it seems to [the person] that he is entirely in another region different*

### DIVINE INSPIRATION

*from this in which we live, where there is shown another light so different from earth's light that if he were to spend his whole life trying to imagine that light, along with the other things, he would be unable to do so. It happens that within an instant so many things together are taught him that if he were to work for many years with his imagination and mind in order to systematize them he wouldn't be able to do so, not with even one-thousandth part of one of them.*

*This is not an intellectual but an imaginative vision, for the eyes of the soul see much better than do bodily eyes here on earth, and without words understanding of some things is given; I mean that if a person sees some saints, he knows them as well as if he had often spoken with them.*[34]

Although many people believe this kind of experience can happen to anyone at any time, the general consensus is that a great deal of preparation must take place. The well-known philosopher, Maimonides (twelfth century) gave specific instruction on this point: "Prophecy is impossible without study and training. When these have created the possibility, then it depends on the will of God whether the possibility is to be turned into reality."[35]

Such study and training include purification, concentration, effort, and mastery. Some traditions also require the study of scripture, fulfillment of precepts, living free of sin, and absolute dedication. Nevertheless, many believe that divine inspiration "can also be attained through deep meditation in prayer. Often it comes automatically through a great act of faith, or from the observance of a commandment [precept] in utter joy."[36]

The Jewish sages teach us that a dream is one-sixtieth of prophecy.[37] This indicates qualities in the dream state parallel to the state of mind in which divine inspiration is received. When we are dreaming, our intellectual faculty is working minimally, while our imagination is running free. Refining and strengthening the imaginative function is a crucial element in our preparation for inspiration. Most of the advice emphasizes the principles that have already been discussed: minimizing excess, dealing with desire and aversion, gaining perspective on the intellectual processes of judgment and comparison, living simply, maintaining integrity, morals, and ethics, and becoming as empty as possible.

Most meditation teachers caution students not to take too seriously visions, voices, and any extrasensory phenomena that occur during intensive practice. This also holds true for dream experiences. Thus a retreatant may ask how to differentiate between an authentic experience of divine inspiration and the busy mind of voices and visions, which may have a quality of prophecy. Even Muhammad was uncertain for a while if his awesome vision had been manipulated by the dark forces. The process of our minds is so intricate, it is often difficult to be certain.

Perhaps the best rule of thumb is to assume self-deception no matter how convincing the experience. The odds overwhelmingly favor the probability that we are simply encountering a delusion. The clarity of our vision cannot be a measure; mentally ill people often have extremely precise hallucinations. Our sense of the truth of the experience cannot be the criterion, nor can we evaluate the message on the basis of its substance.

Eventually we will need to find an experienced teacher for guidance. If we act on our "inspiration" without this objectivity, there is a good chance we will be in error.

Luzzatto gives us instruction in this matter:

> *The main initiation to prophecy . . . depends upon the neophytes'*
> *devotion to God. To the degree that they make themselves worthy*
> *through their deeds and continually purify themselves through . . .*
> *disciplines, they can bring themselves closer and closer to God. The*
> *prophetic influence begins to come to them, and they undergo one*

*experience after another, until they finally attain true prophecy. All this, however, requires the guidance of an experienced prophet. He must have an adequate knowledge of the ways of prophecy, and therefore be able to teach each one what he must do to attain the desired result, depending on the individual's particular level of preparation.*

*When these neophyte prophets begin to experience revelations, the master prophet continues to guide them. On the basis of what is revealed to them, he instructs them and informs them what is still lacking in their quest. Until they attain full prophecy, they require a master for all this. Even though some influence and revelation may have started to come to them, this in itself is not enough to immediately bring them to the ultimate goal. Before they can reach this, they need much guidance and training, each one according to his degree of preparation.*[38]

Today we would use the word *enlightenment* where Luzzatto uses the word *prophecy,* or Enlightened One where he uses Prophet. It is helpful to have a teacher in every phase of the spiritual journey, but frequently we must make our own way. At this level, however, it is not only helpful but imperative to have a guide. Fortunately, when we work hard enough to attain this stage, a teacher almost always manifests, as if by magic. The mystics believe light attracts light in an unknown way; on the spiritual path we receive the guidance we need when we need it.

The experience of divine influence is not discussed much in contemporary spiritual literature despite the fact that Western scripture is full of prophecy. The perspective of the ancient sages is that as long as sadness, depression, and dense thoughts infiltrate our world, enlightenment experiences in the realm of prophecy will be rare while self-delusion will dominate. On the other hand, if we are able to engender a light, soft, joyful state of being, our spiritual work will more likely be imbued with divine inspiration.

# UNION WITH
# THE DIVINE

Most traditions propose that the ultimate source is infinite, unknowable, a great Oneness which is the beginning and end of all existence. This all-encompassing wholeness transcends any concept that particularizes or separates. It is beyond language because all language has limited boundaries. At times, theologians argue over the nature of this Infiniteness; while mystics consider it absurd to use symbols, words, or concepts to try to represent something that even the word *infinite* cannot contain.

Some people maintain that it is impossible to experience complete absorption or annihilation into this wholeness, for there is always a remnant of the part of us which can experience, a spark of the self in its most purified form. Mystics, however, are not concerned with the philosophical or theological level of truth. They believe ultimate truth defies all logic, is paradoxical by definition, and therefore must be discovered in some way other than through the intellect.

The mind is our greatest ally and also our greatest deceiver. The experienced meditator becomes extremely wary of his or her own mind. Repeatedly we notice how rapidly our absolute, unshakable convictions melt away. We experience visions that turn out to be complete fantasy, we have profound insights that upon inspection are actually trivial observations. Although we aspire to truth, we must proceed cautiously through a thicket of self-deception in the hope that we will somehow recognize truth when we find it.

We have good cause for hope. Teresa of Avila teaches us about a state of mind that removes all doubt once and forever. In the following excerpt she is discussing the fifth of seven levels of enlightenment:

> Don't think this union is some kind of dreamy state like the one I mentioned before . . . because even if the experience in the [lower enlightenment state] is abundant, the soul remains doubtful that it was union. It doubts whether it imagined the experience; whether it was asleep; whether the experience was given by God; or whether the devil transformed himself into an angel of light. It is left with a thousand suspicions. . . .
>
> Though there is not so much room for poisonous things to enter [in these lower enlightenment stages], some tiny lizards do enter; since these lizards have slender heads, they can poke their heads in anywhere. And even though they do no harm, especially if one pays no attention to them, they are often a bother since they are little thoughts proceeding from the imagination. . . . But however slender they may be, these little lizards cannot enter this fifth dwelling place; for there is neither imagination, nor memory, nor intellect that can impede this good. And I would dare say that if the prayer is truly union with God the devil cannot even enter or do any damage. His Majesty is so joined and united with the essence of the soul that the devil will not dare approach, nor will he even know about this secret. . . .
>
> This union is above all earthly joys, above all delights, above all consolations, and still more than that. It doesn't matter where those spiritual or earthly joys come from, for the feeling is very different. . . . I once said that the difference is like that between feeling something on the rough outer covering of the body or in the marrow of bones. And that was right on the mark, for I don't know how to say it better.[39]

### PLEASANT MIND STATES

This state occurs beyond our sensory perception and has been described as deathlike, with hardly a breath noticeable. There is nothing here to feel, think, or even experience what is happening. It just happens. At some point, when we literally "come back to our senses," we achieve a realization of an entirely new process and the certainty of a permanent alteration in the perception of ourselves.

How often over the years have we looked in the mirror and wondered, "Is it still me?" The reflection changes a little, a wrinkle here, a gray hair there, but essentially we still look the same—certainly we continue to perceive an intimate familiarity. Sometimes we speculate what it would be like to look in the mirror one day and see somebody else, a completely transformed person, no longer me. Spiritual voyagers report this is precisely what happened when they attained the level of union in the enlightenment process. The alteration was instantaneous and permanent. It was so complete, no room was left for doubt—the previous personality in whom the doubt would have been centered no longer existed. In modern terminology this would be described as psychic chromosomal realignment.

Christian literature is brimming with descriptions of the experience called *unio mystica* (mystical union). It usually marks the pivotal point of an individual's conversion from a sense of separation to a continuous feeling of the presence of the Divine within. The experience is not what we would have thought. In fact, it is usually described in terms of what it is not rather than what it is. Dionysius the Areopagite, sometimes referred to as "the fountainhead of Christian mysticism," described the "absolute truth" as "neither essence, nor eternity, nor time

. . . not even royalty or wisdom, not one, not unity, not divinity or goodness. . . ."[40] Absolute truth cannot be anything we could attribute to it. Therefore, our experience of the state of union is beyond all perception and surely beyond any description.

The well-known Christian mystic Meister Eckhart describes the "still desert of the Godhead" as "where never was seen difference, neither Father, Son, nor Holy Ghost, where there is no one at home, yet where the spark of the soul is more at peace than in itself."[41] There is no one at home! No veils are present here and nothing exists but the primordial light that penetrates all existence and allows us to see to the end of the universe. This is the *visio beatifica,* the ultimate, exquisite inner vision that merges with the essence of creation.

With typical precision, Sufi poets make a distinction between two types of aspirants who experience union. There are those "to whom the Primordial Grace and Loving Kindness has granted salvation after their being submerged in complete union and in the wave of *tauhid* [union], [taking them out] of the belly of the fish [named] 'Annihilation' [placing them] on the shore of separation and in the arena of permanent subsistence [this world], so that they might lead people toward salvation."[42]

This first group are the ones we know. They are those who have reached the highest levels and then, paradoxically, descend again to a place of separation, for they can communicate only if they return to this reality. This process of reentry remains a great mystery. Once we are dwelling in the peace of union, nothing imaginable could pull us back to this world. Yet, the return of these enlightened beings is the only way the rest of us are granted a glimpse of what they have seen. What causes them to tear themselves away from the center of the "All" which has been the dedicated focus of their life's struggle will remain a profound question.

The Sufi poets say that the other group of spiritual adventurers simply disappears. "The others are those who are completely submerged in the ocean of Unity and have been so completely naughted in the belly of the fish [named] 'Annihilation' that never a news or trace comes to the shore of separation and the direction of subsistence . . . the sanctity of perfecting others is not entrusted to them."[43]

There is a controversy in Sufi and other traditions as to which of the two states is "higher." The first is considered the "prophetic" state, which, as we have discussed, is humankind's main vehicle through which the hidden is revealed. The second is more reclusive, and in many ways purer, but we encounter it only through hearsay. Some people believe the prophetic state is higher because it requires an intrinsic strength to return to this reality in order to lead others on the path. The opposing position is that although the "non-returners" do not directly communicate with us, those who dwell in the Unity fulfill the ultimate purpose of creation and thus generate a light that holds the entire universe together.

There need not be a debate on this question when we realize that each is an integral part of the other. The light of the reclusive is essential for the prophet to offer revelation, and the prophet's revelations release the sparks that continue to nourish the Annihilated Ones—neither could exist without the other.

The Buddhist approach to divine union is not too different from Western perspectives. Despite the theological differences between East and West on whether there is a Creator, there remains agreement that there is a divine aspect. This was discussed by Buddhist scholar John Blofeld:

> The difference between God-based religions and those such as Buddhism and Taoism, which are, to coin a term, god-free is to some extent a verbal one. In the former, supreme divinity is conceived as a being, in the latter—as a state. Now, where space and form are transcended and we are considering an invisible, omnipresent source of blessedness, the difference between a being and a state of being is obviously hard to define. The link between the two concepts is provided by the Christian mystics' recognition that even God (as a being) is subordinate to the Godhead (a state). In the sādhana [spiritual discipline], the empowerment and purification come from the union of the individual (temporarily drawn out of his puny egohood) with the divine Source which is the shining Void.[44]

The spirit of divine union dissolves all types of distinction. Once we have entered the pure realm of Oneness that is No-Thingness, differentiation ceases to exist. Rabbi Abraham Isaac Kook (1865–1935) spoke out strongly on this question in his discussion of the bickering and backbiting that takes place between adherents of different faiths.

> One of the greatest afflictions of man's spiritual world is that every discipline of knowledge, every feeling, impedes the emergence of [every] other. The result is that most people remain limited and one-sided, and their shortcomings are continually on the increase. The cloud that each discipline casts on the other also leads the devotee of a particular discipline to feel a sharp antagonism toward the discipline that is remote to him, whose values are outside his concerns. This defect cannot continue permanently. Man's nobler future is destined to come, when he will develop to a sound spiritual state so that instead of each discipline negating the other, all knowledge, all feeling will be envisioned from any branch of it.

*This is precisely the true nature of reality. No spiritual phenom-enon can stand independently. Each is inter-penetrated by all. Only the limitations of our mental capacities impede us from glimpsing those aspects of the spiritual domain that are imminent in every part of it. When man rises in his spiritual development his eyes will open to see properly. "Then the blind will see and the deaf will hear, and the earth will be full of the knowledge of the Lord as the waters cover the sea." (Isa. 35:5, 11:9)*[45]

As with all the stages of enlightenment, unification requires a strong foundation to integrate it. A kabbalistic principle says the light is always present, but we must work to build a vessel to hold it. Occasionally we may experience the true light before our vessel is ready. When that happens, a frequent experience for many, the light is recognized only as a passing phenomenon. In some instances the light is too powerful and we shatter, suffer-ing physical or mental breakdown. In Hindu terminol-ogy, this is known as raising the *kundalinī* before we are ready.

One way of building the vessel of divine union is to focus on the unity of all existence. In this process, we dissolve all barriers that present themselves, whether they be obvious barriers of ignorance that raise prejudice and discrimination, or subtle barriers of distinction, compar-ison, and judging. Anything that has a quality of separa-tion must be viewed through the lens of union.

Joseph Karo, the sixteenth-century mystic who had an interior guiding voice known as a *maggid*, recorded the *maggid*'s advice in this way:

*This is what a person must do: He must integrate all of his thoughts toward the fear of God and His worship. . . . This should certainly be true when you pray. Nullify every thought that enters your heart. . . . Unify your heart constantly, at all times, so that every instant you will think of nothing other than God, his Torah and His worship. This is the mystery of Unity, through which a person literally unifies himself with his Creator. The soul attaches itself to Him, and becomes one with Him, so that the body literally becomes a dwelling place of the Divine Presence. This is what the Torah means when it says, "You shall fear God your Lord, and you shall serve Him and attach yourself to Him." (Deuteronomy 10:20)*[46]

The experience of union was frequently sensual or filled with a love that transcended mundane expression. A Sufi love poem catches this spirit exquisitely:

> *I have separated my heart from this world,*
> *My heart and Thou are not separate.*
> *And when slumber closes my eyes,*
> *I find Thee between the eye and the lid.*[47]

When the Sufis attained these levels of awareness, they were extremely self-demanding, maintaining integrity in the subtlest points. The ninth-century Sufi Bāyezīd Bistāmī's yearning was so intense, he sometimes fainted when uttering the call to prayer, but he always understated his experiences or gave them a strange twist. He described what took place as follows:

*As soon as I attained to His Unity I became a bird with a body of Oneness and wings of Everlastingness, and I continued flying in the air of Quality for ten years, until I reached an atmosphere a million times as large, and I flew on, until I found myself in the field of Eternity and I saw there the Tree of Oneness. . . . And I looked, and I knew that all this was a cheat.*[48]

Wherever we look in spiritual literature, we find superlatives extolling the magnificence of ultimate truth. Among some of the Sufis, however, we detect a mixture of ecstasy and tears. Bistāmī was capable of saying "Praise be to Me, how great is My Majesty!" He is said to have reached a state of emptiness until he had touched "at least for a moment, the world of absolute unity where, as he said, lover, beloved, and love are one, and where he himself is the wine, the wine-drinker, and the cup-bearer."[49]

We know that this state has aspects of sublime peace, absolute clarity, undivided joy, and crystalline certainty, but it also has aspects of distress, anguish, and sorrow, which come from the awareness that we cannot be unified as long as we remain in our body. Not only are we ultimately limited ourselves, we see the true nature of separation and the pervasive suffering of the rest of creation.

Despite this, almost all mystics express an unshakable optimism. The true nature of creation is bittersweet, but the experience of union with the divine source, in whatever measure, carries with it a sense of the perfection of all aspects of creation. Everything works with the precision of a divine orchestra. The quieter our minds, the more we can take it all in. Then everything is beautiful, including the bitter side.

The ancient Upanishads teach us "that are thou." We cannot separate ourselves from anything. Some say that the gift we have of intellectual capacity is our greatest liability. Our facility to think with discrimination has as its by-product a feeling of separation—this is what has removed us from the Garden of Eden. If we are able to let go of this separation and alienation, we will become aware that we have been in the Garden all along without realizing it. This is the hidden truth of divine union, the recognition that everything is a part of us, that we do not really exist as we think we are. Every aspect of separation comes from deluded thinking. The Upanishads are explicit on this point:

### UNION WITH THE DIVINE

*Know God, and all fetters will be losed. Ignorance will vanish.*
*Birth, death, and rebirth will be no more. Meditate upon him and*
*transcend physical consciousness. Thus will you reach union with*
*the lord of the universe. Thus will you become identified with him*
*who is One without a second. In him all your desires will find*
*fulfillment. The truth is that you are always united with the Lord.*
*But you must* know *this. Nothing further is there to know.*
*Meditate, and you will realize that mind, matter, and māyā (the*
*power which unites mind and matter) are but three aspects of*
*Brahman, the one reality.*[50]

Even if we have not developed the concentration and
strength to maintain a sense of union for an extended
period, even a glimpse into this Garden is sufficient to
empower us to continue on the spiritual path for the rest
of our lives. We can say these words and maybe even feel
a sense of their truth, but once we experience the sense of
divine union, a flood washes through us and we are never
again the same. From that time forward, we have no
choice but to follow the path that unfolds. It is a path of
ever-increasing awareness.

# THE FIFTH DIMENSION

Basic Kabbalah describes the creation in terms of five dimensions. The first three are the height, width, and breadth that we know as space. The fourth is time. The fifth dimension is the spiritual plane. It has qualities that transcend time and space. When we enter this plane, the entire universe of spiritual phenomena becomes instantly available. There is no traveling from place to place, because there is no space. There is no waiting for anything, because there is no time. Each instant is complete; all communion is absolute; there are no limits; all thought is useless; every aspect of creation is perfect.

People who have entered this realm have reported amazing things. When we try to describe them, our words become corrupted in the attempt to define the intangible and ephemeral. Words like Cosmic Consciousness, God-realization, True Enlightenment, and Utter Illumination all aim to encapsulate the infinite. Nonetheless, as the soul within each of us cries out in loneliness, constantly urging us to return to its source, we imbibe descriptions of the spiritual dimension as sweet nectar, praying fervently that they are true.

As we deepen our spiritual explorations, we become more adept in distinguishing true accounts from those that are false. Each time we have a personal experience in the fifth dimension, we resonate with others who have had similar experiences. Thus our attunement is refined and we are able to perceive the authenticity of transmissions.

All traditions have a stage where one transcends the mundane into a state of enormously expanded awareness. The levels of equanimity, divine inspiration, and union are all part of this transformation. Even though we isolate them for purposes of description, they really blend into one another as the enlightenment process reaches the highest stage, a permanent absorption into the fifth dimension.

The words *consciousness* and *awareness* fall short at this point because this level of "knowing" is in no way intellectual. Our main difficulty with the idea of cosmic consciousness is that we do not really understand mundane consciousness. As Gurdjieff pointed out:

> Moments of consciousness are very short and are separated by long intervals of completely unconscious, mechanical working . . . you can think, feel, act, speak, work, without being conscious of it. . . . [The] principal mistake consists in thinking that you always have consciousness. . . . In reality consciousness is a property which is continually changing. Now it is present, now it is not present.[51]

Most of our lives, according to Gurdjieff, are not spent in consciousness, but in a mechanical mode. Yet, even though we may be acting mechanically, we are still not operating as machines. A component of everything we do is on a level of "knowing." We may be fulfilling a rote function on an assembly line, our minds may be filled with fantasy, but a part of us "knows" exactly what we are doing and what we are thinking at all times.

We can all relate to this mysterious "knowing" that

transcends consciousness. It is the link that connects us with the fifth dimension. When we are accomplished enough in our spiritual practice to break through the veils of illusion, this "knowing" expands, our practice strengthens, and the process feeds itself.

During the times in our practice when we stand just inside the entrance of the fifth dimension, we constantly engage the unfolding of truth. Indeed, the fifth dimension is the abode of our "knowing." We often feel that we are remembering something forgotten rather than acquiring something new. This is our spiritual home.

A few people become so intensely integrated with this timelessness that they assimilate it in a way that releases them from the grip of the four dimensions of this world. In his classic book *Cosmic Consciousness*, R. M. Bucke offers a broad definition of this state of being:

> Along with the consciousness of the cosmos there occurs an intellectual enlightenment of illumination which alone would place the individual on a new plane of existence—would make him almost a member of a new species. To this is added a state of moral exaltation, an indescribable feeling of elevation, elation, and joyousness, and a quickening of the moral sense. . . . With these come what may be called a sense of immortality, a consciousness of eternal life, not a conviction that he shall have this, but the consciousness that he has it already.[52]

It is fascinating that Bucke identifies this illumined being as a "new species." Most of us approach enlightenment in this way, as if a transmutation takes place, despite the fact that almost all teachers point out that anything we can attain is already part of our essential nature. They insist that entry into the fifth dimension is not the birth of a new being, but a return to our original, true nature.

Swami Vivekananda called this deeper wisdom the "superconscious":

### THE FIFTH DIMENSION

*The mind itself has a higher state of existence, beyond reason, a superconscious state, and when the mind gets to that higher state, then this knowledge beyond reasoning comes. . . . There is no feeling of "I," and yet the mind works, desireless, free from restlessness, objectless, bodiless. Then the Truth shines in its full effulgence, and we know ourselves—for samādhi lies potential in us all—for what we truly are, free, immortal, omnipotent . . . identical with the Ātman or Universal Soul.*[53]

Our efforts in practice are toward revealing the enormous potential that already exists within us. This is done by starving those aspects of ourselves that tend to trick us into believing we are something other than our true enlightened nature. There is nothing to acquire outside ourselves and we do not have to be transformed into a new breed. Strip away the illusion and we are left with full liberation.

Ramana Maharshi teaches us:

*Truly there is no cause for you to be miserable and unhappy. You yourself impose limitations on your true nature of infinite Being, and then weep that you are but a finite creature. Then you take up this or that sādhana [spiritual practice] to transcend the nonexistent limitations. But if your sādhana itself assumes the existence of the limitations, how can it help you to transcend them? Hence I say know that you are really the infinite, pure Being, the Self Absolute. You are always that Self and nothing but that Self.*[54]

It is all so simple. Yet, it takes significant effort to attain this simplicity. A teacher can help us in the process, but enlightenment is not something that can be given. How can we receive what we already have?

We know it can be done. We can read accounts in all traditions of those who made this journey, and this encourages us in the knowledge that a high level in the enlightenment process is attainable. It is not a myth.

PLEASANT MIND STATES

Every spiritual seeker has the potential to enter the fifth dimension.

Philip Kapleau records a wonderful account of a great enlightenment experience by a young woman named Yaeko:

> *Buddhas and patriarchs haven't deceived me! I have seen my Face before my parents were born clearer than a diamond in the palm of my hand. The absolute truth of every word of the patriarchs and the sutras has appeared before my eyes with crystal clarity. . . .*[55]

The account goes on to show how she came to understand that even this enlightenment experience had a potential corrupting element. If we become attached to any level of enlightenment, this can generate an "awful smell." No matter how far we go in this process, we must remain alert to the slightest indication of ego-identification.

Chögyam Trungpa offers a Tibetan Buddhist perspective of the higher dimension in his description of the *bodhisattva*:

> *The bodhisattva never seeks a trance state, bliss, or absorption. He is simply awake to life situations as they are. He is particularly aware of the continuity of meditation with generosity, morality, patience, and energy. There is a continual feeling of "awake."*[56]

The fifth dimension of spirituality is not a level to which we must aspire, it pervades all life. Each step we make along the path simply deepens our awareness of this. It is as though we plan to walk to a store to buy a bottle of perfume without realizing that we are constantly breathing a marvelous scent each and every moment. As long as we are searching for a store to buy our perfume, we miss the flowers along the way. Once we connect with and are attuned to each instant, we become dazzled by the richness and intensity of life.

We do not have to read the accounts of mystics to appreciate the grandeur of the spiritual realm; we merely have to stop and look. It does not matter where we are in any moment, it is here with us, right now. Stop. Be silent. Take a breath. Notice everything that is happening without trying to hold on to any of it. Everything we ever wanted spiritually is right here in this fifth dimension.

The scriptures are filled with the riches of the spiritual realm. Many paradigms of enlightenment experiences exist in Western tradition. The Book of Daniel, for example, expresses many different visions and prophecies. Some of the visions are explained to Daniel by angels while others are too enigmatic. As we read through this book, we gain a sense of what life would be like dwelling in the fifth dimension, constantly experiencing marvelous visions and fearful prophecies:

*In the third year of Koresh king of Paras a thing was revealed to Daniel . . . and the word was true . . . and he understood the thing and had understanding of the vision. In those days I Daniel was mourning three full weeks [because of this vision]. I ate no pleasant bread nor did meat or wine come into my mouth, nor did I anoint myself at all, till three whole weeks were fulfilled.*

*And on the twenty-fourth day of the first month, as I was by the side of the great river. . . . I lifted up my eyes, and looked, and behold a certain man clothed in linen, whose loins were girded with fine gold of Ufaz: his body also was like the beryl, and his face like the appearance of lightning, and his eyes like torches of fire, and his arms and his feet in colour like burnished brass, and the sound of his words like the voice of a multitude. And I Daniel alone saw the vision: for the men who were with me did not see the vision; but a great trembling fell upon them, so that they fled to hide themselves. So I was left alone, and saw this great vision, and there remained no strength in me. . . . And, behold, a hand touched me, which set me trembling on my knees and on the palms of my hands. And he said to me, O Daniel, thou man greatly beloved, understand the*

PLEASANT MIND STATES

*words that I speak to thee, and stand upright: for to thee am I now*
*sent. . . . Then he said to me, Fear not, Daniel: for from the first*
*day that thou didst set thy heart to understand and to humble thyself*
*before thy God, thy words were heard, and I am come because of thy*
*words.*[57]

*Then I said, O my Lord, what shall be the end of these things?*
*And he said, Go thy way, Daniel: for the words are closed up and*
*sealed till the time of the end. Many shall purify themselves and*
*make themselves white, and be tried; but the wicked shall do*
*wickedly: and none of the wicked shall understand; but the wise*
*shall understand.*[58]

The understanding of the wise is not anything that we
would imagine. Paradox reigns supreme in the realm of
the fifth dimension. We have seen that it takes concentration, effort, purification, and mastery to pursue the
spiritual path, but we have also seen that striving and
desire are self-defeating. The wisdom of spiritual passage
is not something that can be transmitted through language or logic, yet we *can* attain wisdom as many have
before us—it is our birthright.

We close this book with a final quote that sums up the
wisdom of the enlightenment process as an enigmatic
teaching. This teaching is epitomized in the smile of the
Buddha, who holds the secret and is willing to share it,
but who knows how difficult it is to learn. May we all be
blessed to have the secret unfold within us, grow on the
path of wisdom, taste its delicious fruits, open our hearts,
expand our awareness, and dissolve into the timeless,
spaceless realm of ultimate truth.

*The* bodhisattva *Subhūti said: "Profound, O Venerable One,*
*is the perfect Transcendental Wisdom."*

*And the Venerable One replied: "Abysmally profound, like the*
*space of the universe, O Subhūti, is the perfect Transcendental*
*Wisdom."*

### THE FIFTH DIMENSION

*Subhūti said again: "Difficult to be attained through Awakening is the perfect Transcendental Wisdom, O Venerable One."*

*To which the Venerable One replied: "That is the reason, O Subhūti, why no one ever attains it through Awakening."*[59]

# NOTES

## NOTES FOR "MASTERING MONKEY MIND"

1. Thomas Merton, *The Asian Journal of Thomas Merton,* ed. Naomi Burton, Brother Patrick Hart, and James Laughlin (New York: New Directions, 1968) pp. 389–90.

2. Philip Kapleau, *The Three Pillars of Zen* (New York: Anchor/Doubleday, 1966) p. 377.

3. Ibid., p. 369.

4. Ibid., p. 61.

5. Paramahansa Yogananda, *Autobiography of a Yogi* (Los Angeles: Self Realization Fellowship, 1975) p. 126n.

6. Ibid., p. 278.

7. Ibid.

8. Ajahn Chah, *A Taste of Freedom* (Ubon Rajathani, Thailand: The Sangha, Bung Wai Forest Monastery, 1980) p. 5.

9. Kapleau, *Three Pillars of Zen,* p. 376.

10. Paul Reps, *Zen Flesh, Zen Bones* (Garden City, New York: Anchor/Doubleday, 1957) pp. 42–43.

11. Edward Conze, *Buddhism: Its Essence and Development* (New York: Harper & Row, 1975) pp. 104–5.

## NOTES FOR "THE FOUNDATION OF SPIRITUAL PRACTICE"

1. Bhikkhu Suruttama, *Buddhist America,* ed. Don Morreale (Santa Fe, New Mexico: John Muir Publications, 1988) p. 10.

NOTES

2. John Bennett, *Long Pilgrimage* (Clearlake, California: Dawn Horse Press, 1983) p. 95.

3. Paramahansa Yogananda, *Autobiography of a Yogi* (Los Angeles: Self Realization Fellowship, 1975) pp. 262–3.

4. Annemarie Schimmel, *Mystical Dimensions of Islam* (Chapel Hill: University of North Carolina Press, 1978) p. 241.

5. Ibid., p. 243.

6. Bertrand Russell, *History of Western Philosophy* (London: Unwin Paperbacks, 1980) p. 51.

7. Ibid.

8. Louis Jacobs, *Jewish Mystical Testimonies* (New York: Schocken Books, 1977) p. 156*n*.

9. Yogananda, *Autobiography of a Yogi,* pp. 562–63.

10. Ibid.

11. Taiko Yamasaki, *Shingon: Japanese Esoteric Buddhism,* trans. Richard and Cynthia Peterson (Boston/London: Shambhala, 1988) p. 189.

12. David Godman, ed., *Be As You Are: The Teachings of Sri Ramana Maharshi* (New York and London: Arkana, 1985) p. 100. It should be noted that a more common definition for *guru* is "dispeller of darkness," from *gu,* "darkness" and *ru,* "that which dispels." Yogananda, *Autobiography of a Yogi,* p. 3.

13. Ajahn Chah, *A Still Forest Pool,* ed. Jack Kornfield and Paul Breiter (Wheaton, Illinois: Theosophical Publishing House, 1985) pp. 150–1.

14. *Avoda Zara* 20b, Babylonian Talmud. See also Moses Hayim Luzzatto, *The Path of the Just,* trans. Shraga Silverstein (Jerusalem: Feldheim, 1980). The entire book is a discussion of these higher plateaus of enlightenment.

15. Prov. 24:30–34.

16. Luzzatto, *Path of the Just,* p. 76*n*.

17. Fritz Meier, "The Transformation of Man in Mystical Islam," in *Man and Transformation,* ed. Joseph Campbell (Princeton, New Jersey: Bollingen Series, Princeton University Press, 1980) p. 45.

18. Ibid.

19. Paul Reps, *Zen Flesh, Zen Bones* (Garden City, New York: Anchor/Doubleday, 1957) p. 75.

20. Ibid.

21. Philip Kapleau, *The Three Pillars of Zen* (New York: Anchor/Doubleday, 1966) pp. 56–57.

22. Ibid.

23. Godman, ed., *Be As You Are: The Teachings of Sri Ramana Maharshi*, p. 223.

24. Thomas Carlyle, *Sartor Resartus* (London/Melbourne: Everyman's Library, John M. Dent & Sons, 1984).

25. William James, *The Varieties of Religious Experience* (New York: Viking Penguin, 1982) p. 212.

26. Ibid., p. 223.

27. The word *haprishut* means "retreat," "separation," and "withdrawal." The popular translation by Shraga Silverstein of Luzzatto's *The Path of the Just* uses the word *separation* for *haprishut*. However, *separation* is most often used to indicate an aspect of alienation, being so caught up in oneself that a barrier separates you from everything else. Luzzatto's use of the word is more positive, that you willingly separate from corrupting influences in order to open a clear channel to the Divine Source. Therefore, to minimize confusion, the word *withdrawal* will be substituted to imply a willful act.

28. Luzzatto, *Path of the Just*, p. 179.

29. Ibid., p. 201.

30. Schimmel, *Mystical Dimensions of Islam*, p. 365.

31. Chah, *A Still Forest Pool*, pp. 112–13.

32. Yogananda, *Autobiography of a Yogi*, p. 238.

33. Luzzatto, *Path of the Just*, p. 201.

## NOTES FOR "UNPLEASANT MIND STATES"

1. John Bennett, *Long Pilgrimage* (Clearlake, California: Dawn Horse Press, 1983) p. 41.

2. J. Krishnamurti, *Think on These Things* (New York: Harper & Row, 1970) p. 30.

3. Gershom Scholem, *Major Trends in Jewish Mysticism* (New York: Schocken Books, 1946) p. 123.

4. Ibid., p. 96.

5. Nachman of Breslov, *Advice*, collected by Rabbi Nathan

of Breslov, trans. Avraham Greenbaum (Jerusalem: Breslov Research Institute, 1983) p. 246.

6. Fritz Meier, "Transformation of Man in Mystical Islam," in *Man and Transformation,* ed. Joseph Campbell (Princeton, New Jersey: Bollingen Series, Princeton University Press, 1980) p. 52.

7. Philip Kapleau, *The Three Pillars of Zen* (New York: Anchor/Doubleday, 1966) p. 346.

8. Ibid.

9. Mircea Eliade, "Mystery and Spiritual Regeneration," in *Man and Transformation,* ed. Campbell, p. 18.

10. P. D. Ouspensky, *In Search of the Miraculous* (New York: Harcourt, Brace & World, 1949) p. 274.

11. Aryeh Kaplan, *Meditation and Kabbalah* (York Beach, Maine: Samuel Weiser, 1986) p. 294.

12. Kapleau, *The Three Pillars of Zen,* p. 245.

13. Ibid.

14. Ibid., p. 249.

15. Louis Finkelstein, *Akiba* (New York: Atheneum, 1981) p. 276.

16. Ibid., pp. 276–77.

17. David Godman, ed., *Be As You Are: The Teachings of Sri Ramana Maharshi* (New York and London: Arkana, 1985) p. 173. The word *One* has been inserted where Ramana Maharshi uses the word *Self* to avoid confusing readers. Ramana Maharshi's *Self,* with a capital *S,* is clearly distinct from the idea of self that relates to the ego.

18. J. Krishnamurti, *Think on These Things,* p. 259.

19. William James, *The Varieties of Religious Experience* (New York: Viking Penguin, 1982) p. 275.

20. Exod. 1:21

21. Quoted in Louis Jacobs, *Hasidic Thought* (New York: Behrman House, 1976) p. 204.

22. Ibid., p. 204.

23. Kaplan, *Meditation and Kabbalah,* p. 286.

24. *Pirke Avot* 1:4

25. *Pirke Avot* 1:7

26. Eliade, "Mystery and Spiritual Regeneration," p. 18.

## NOTES

27. Hal Stone and Sidra Winkelman, *Embracing Our Selves* (San Rafael, California: New World Library, 1989) p. 27*n*.

28. James, *The Varieties of Religious Experience,* p. 275.

29. Anonymous, *The Cloud of Unknowing,* trans. Clifton Wolters (Harmondsworth, Middlesex, England: Penguin Books, 1961) p. 90.

30. Thomas Merton, trans., *The Wisdom of the Desert* (New York: New Directions, 1960) p. 45.

31. D. Ben-Amos & J. R. Mintz, *In Praise of the Baal Shem Tov* (New York: Schocken Books, 1970) p. 200.

32. Ram Dass, *Journey of Awakening* (New York: Bantam Books, 1985) p. 173.

33. Kapleau, *The Three Pillars of Zen,* p. 352.

34. Godman, ed., *Be As You Are: The Teachings of Sri Ramana Maharshi,* pp. 173–74.

35. Annemarie Schimmel, *Mystical Dimensions of Islam* (Chapel Hill: University of North Carolina Press, 1978) pp. 114–15.

36. Ibid.

37. In Jewish mysticism, there is a study of *gematria* where each letter of the Hebrew alphabet has a value. When different words have equal values it is an indication of an essential connection. Amalek is spelled: *ayin* (70), *mem* (40), *lamed* (30), and *kuf* (100). *Suffek* is spelled: *samek* (60), *peh* (80), *kuf* (100). They both add up to 240.

38. James, *The Varieties of Religious Experience,* p. 506.

39. Kapleau, *The Three Pillars of Zen,* p. 64.

40. The Baal Shem Tov was Rebbe Nachman's great grand-father.

41. Adin Steinsaltz, *Beggars and Prayers* (New York: Basic Books, 1979) p. 113*n*; see also Arnold Band, *Nachman of Bratslav* (New York: Paulist Press, 1978) p. 139*n*.

42. Ibid.

## NOTES FOR "PLEASANT MIND STATES"

1. Thomas Merton, trans., *The Wisdom of the Desert* (New York: New Directions, 1960) p. 54.

NOTES

2. Philip Kapleau, *The Three Pillars of Zen* (New York: Anchor/Doubleday, 1966) p. 216.

3. Annemarie Schimmel, *Mystical Dimensions of Islam* (Chapel Hill: University of North Carolina Press, 1978) p. 178.

4. Kapleau, *The Three Pillars of Zen,* p. 256.

5. David Godman, ed., *Be As You Are: The Teachings of Sri Ramana Maharshi* (New York and London: Arkana, 1985) p. 174.

6. John Bennett, *Long Pilgrimage* (Clearlake, California: Dawn Horse Press, 1983) p. 82.

7. The Song of Songs 2:8–13

8. St. John of the Cross, *Spiritual Canticle,* trans. and ed. E. Allison Peers (New York: Image Books/Doubleday, 1961) stanzas 13–18, pp. 44–45.

9. Ben Zion Bokser, trans., *Abraham Isaac Kook* (New York: Paulist Press, 1978) p. 227.

10. Pierre Teilhard de Chardin, *The Future of Man* (New York: Harper & Row, 1964) p. 301.

11. Gershom Scholem, *Major Trends in Jewish Mysticism* (New York: Schocken Books, 1946) p. 95.

12. Ibid.

13. Schimmel, *Mystical Dimensions of Islam,* p. 39.

14. Ibid., pp. 165–66.

15. Burton Watson, trans., *The Complete Works of Chuang Tzu* (New York: Columbia University Press, 1968) p. 69.

16. Aryeh Kaplan, *Meditation and the Bible* (York Beach, Maine: Samuel Weiser, 1978) p. 87.

17. Kapleau, *The Three Pillars of Zen,* p. 360.

18. Godman, ed., *Be As You Are: The Teachings of Sri Ramana Maharshi,* p. 160.

19. Rabbi Yehuda L. Ashlag, *Talmud Esser Sfirot,* trans. Rabbi Levi I. Krakovsky (Old City, Jerusalem: Yeshivat Kol Yehuda) pp. 14–28.

20. Rabbi Moses Cordovero, *The Palm Tree of Deborah,* trans. Louis Jacobs (New York: Sepher-Hermon Press, 1981) p. 46.

21. Thomas Keating, *The Mystery of Christ* (Shaftesbury, England: Element Books, 1987) p. 106.

22. Thomas Merton, *The Asian Journal of Thomas Merton,* ed.

Naomi Burton, Brother Patrick Hart, and James Laughlin (New York: New Directions, 1968) p. 120.

23. Ibid., p. 280.

24. William James, *The Varieties of Religious Experience* (New York: Viking Penguin, 1982) p. 248.

25. Ibid.

26. Quoted in Ibid., pp. 248–49.

27. Ramana Maharshi, *The Spiritual Teaching of Ramana Maharshi* (Boulder/London: Shambhala, 1972) p. 83.

28. William Johnston, ed., *The Cloud of Unknowing* (New York: Image/Doubleday, 1973) pp. 136–37.

29. Moshe Chayim Luzzatto, *The Way of God,* trans. Aryeh Kaplan (Jerusalem/New York: Feldheim, 1983) pp. 204–5.

30. Aryeh Kaplan, *The Handbook of Jewish Thought* (New York/Jerusalem: Maznaim, 1979) pp. 83–97.

31. Aryeh Kaplan, *Meditation and Kabbalah* (York Beach, Maine: Samuel Weiser, 1986) p. 82.

32. Schimmel, *Mystical Dimensions of Islam,* p. 161.

33. Ibid., pp. 407–8.

34. Teresa of Avila, *The Interior Castle,* trans. K. Kavanaugh and O. Rodriguez (New York: Paulist Press, 1979) pp. 135–36.

35. Maimonides, *Guide of the Perplexed,* trans. M. Friedlander (New York: Hebrew Publishing) Part 2, chapter 32:3, p. 164.

36. Kaplan, *Handbook of Jewish Thought,* p. 90.

37. *Berakoth* 57b

38. Luzzatto, *The Way of God,* pp. 215–17.

39. Teresa of Avila, *The Interior Castle,* pp. 86–89.

40. James, *The Varieties of Religious Experience,* p. 416.

41. Ibid., p. 417.

42. Schimmel, *Mystical Dimensions of Islam,* p. 6.

43. Ibid.

44. John Blofeld, *The Tantric Mysticism of Tibet* (Boston: Shambhala, 1987) pp. 213–14.

45. Bokser, trans., *Abraham Isaac Kook,* pp. 195–96.

46. Quoted in Kaplan, *Meditation and Kabbalah,* pp. 177–78.

47. Schimmel, *Mystical Dimensions of Islam,* p. 62.

48. Ibid., p. 49.

49. Ibid.

228

50. Swami Prabhavananda, trans., *The Upanishads* (Hollywood, California: Vedanta Press, 1957) Book 12, *Svetasvatara,* p. 119.

51. P. D. Ouspensky, *In Search of the Miraculous* (New York: Harcourt, Brace & World, 1949) pp. 116–17.

52. R. M. Bucke, *Cosmic Consciousness* (New York: E. P. Dutton, 1969) p. 3.

53. Quoted in James, *The Varieties of Religious Experience,* p. 400.

54. Ramana Maharshi, *The Spiritual Teachings,* p. 92.

55. Kapleau, *The Three Pillars of Zen,* p. 290.

56. Chögyam Trungpa, *Cutting Through Spiritual Materialism* (Berkeley: Shambhala, 1973) p. 177.

57. Dan. 10:1–12

58. Dan. 12:8–10

59. Joseph Campbell, *The Masks of God: Oriental Mythology* (New York: Viking Press, 1962) p. 303.

# RECOMMENDED READING
# FOR RETREATANTS

The following is a selected list of books that are particularly inspiring or that contain helpful descriptions of retreat practices. The list is limited to books that have been read by or recommended to the author. However, there are thousands of other titles that have inspired spiritual seekers over the centuries. If a book has been omitted that a reader has found to be special in his or her life, suggestions are welcome.

Anonymous. Johnston, William, ed. *The Cloud of Unknowing*. New York: Doubleday, 1973.

Arberry, A. J. *Sufism*. New York: Harper & Row, 1950.

———. *Muslim Saints and Mystics*. Oxon, England: Routledge and Kegan Paul, 1966.*

Attar, Fariduddin. *The Conference of the Birds*. Berkeley: Shambhala, 1971.

Augustine, Saint. *Confessions*. New York: Viking Penguin, 1961.

Baldick, Julian. *Mystical Islam*. New York: New York University Press, 1989.

Behari, Bankey. *Sufis, Mystics and Yogis of India*. Bombay, India: Bhavan's Book University, 1962.*

Bennett, John G. *Long Pilgrimage*. Clearlake, California: Dawn Horse Press, 1983.

Ben-Amos, D. and Mintz, J. R. *In Praise of the Baal Shem Tov*. New York: Schocken Books, 1970.

* Esoteric books from small publishing houses may be available through special mail order. An excellent resource is: Yes! Books & Videos, P.O. Box 10726, Arlington, VA 22210.

#### RECOMMENDED READING

Boehme, Jacob. *Mysterium Magnum*. London: Watkins, 1924.*

Bokser, Ben Zion. *Abraham Isaac Kook*. New York: Paulist Press, 1978.

———. *The Jewish Mystical Tradition*. New York: Pilgrim Press, 1981.

Bourke, Vernon J., ed. *The Essential Augustine*. Indianapolis, Indiana: Hackett Publishing, 1974.

Brown, Raphael, trans. *The Little Flowers of St. Francis*. Garden City, New York: Doubleday, 1958.

Buber, Martin, comp. Translated by Esther Cameron. Edited by Paul Mendes-Flohr. *Ecstatic Confessions*. San Francisco: Harper & Row, 1985.

———. *The Legend of the Baal-Shem*. New York: Schocken Books, 1955.

———. *Tales of the Hasidim* (2 vols.). New York: Schocken Books), 1947.

Chah, Ven. Ajahn. *A Still Forest Pool*. Edited by Jack Kornfield and Paul Breiter. Wheaton, Illinois: The Theosophical Publishing House, 1985.*

———. *A Taste of Freedom*. Thailand: Bung Wai Forest Monastery, 1980.*

Chittick, William C. *The Sufi Path of Love: The Spiritual Teachings of Rumi*. Albany: State University of New York Press, 1983.

Chögyam Trungpa. *Cutting Through Spiritual Materialism*. Edited by John Baker and Marvin Casper. Berkeley: Shambhala, 1973.

———. *The Myth of Freedom*. Berkeley: Shambhala, 1976.

Cordovero, Rabbi Moses. *The Palm Tree of Deborah*. Translated by Louis Jacobs. New York: Sepher-Hermon Press, 1974.

Deshimaru, Taisen. *Questions to a Zen Master*. Translated by Nancy Amphoux. New York: E. P. Dutton, 1985.

Dionysius the Areopagite. *The Divine Names*. Surrey, England: Shrine of Wisdom, 1957.*

Faris, Amin Nabih, trans. *The Mysteries of Purity*. Lahore, India: Muhammad Ashraf, 1966.*

Foster, R. J. *Celebration of Discipline: The Path to Spiritual Growth*. New York: Harper & Row, 1978.

RECOMMENDED READING

Ginzberg, Louis. *The Legends of the Jews* (6 vols.). Philadelphia: Jewish Publication Society of America, 1982.

Godman, David, ed. *Be As You Are: The Teachings of Sri Ramana Maharshi*. London and New York: Arkana, 1985.

Goldstein, Joseph. *The Experience of Insight*. Boston: Shambhala, 1983.

Goldstein, Joseph and Jack Kornfield. *Seeking the Heart of Wisdom: The Path of Insight Meditation*. Boston and London: Shambhala, 1987.

Goleman, Daniel. *Varieties of the Meditative Experience*. New York: E. P. Dutton, 1977. Reissued under the title *The Meditative Mind* (Jeremy Tarcher, 1987).

Govinda, Anagarika. *Foundations of Tibetan Mysticism, According to the Esoteric Teachings of the Great Mantra, Om Mani Padme Hum*. New York: Samuel Weiser, 1970.

Herrigel, Eugen. *Zen in the Art of Archery*. New York: Pantheon Books, 1953.

Heschel, Abraham. *The Sabbath*. New York: Farrar, Straus & Giroux, 1951.

Ignatius, Saint. *The Spiritual Exercises of St. Ignatius*. Translated by Anthony Mottola.

Jacobs, Louis. *Hasidic Prayer*. New York: Schocken Books, 1972.
————. *Hasidic Thought*. New York: Behrman House, 1976.

James, William. *The Varieties of Religious Experience*. New York: Viking Penguin, 1982.

John of the Cross, Saint. *Spiritual Canticle*. Translated by E. Allison Peers. New York: Image Books/Doubleday, 1961.

Kadowaki, J. K. *Zen and the Bible*. Translated by Joan Rieck. London and New York: Arkana, 1989.

Kaplan, Aryeh. *Inner Space: Introduction to Kabbalah, Meditation, and Prophecy*. Edited by Abraham Sutton. Jerusalem: Moznaim Publishing, 1990.
————. *Meditation and the Bible*. York Beach, Maine: Samuel Weiser, 1981.
————. *Meditation and Kabbalah*. York Beach, Maine: Samuel Weiser, 1986.
————, trans. *Rabbi Nachman's Wisdom*. New York: Sepher-Hermon, 1973.

## RECOMMENDED READING

Kapleau, Philip. *The Three Pillars of Zen*. Garden City, New York: Anchor/Doubleday, 1966.

Keating, Thomas. *The Mystery of Christ: The Liturgy as a Spiritual Experience*. Rockport, Massachusetts: Element Books, 1991.

Khan, Hazrat Inayat. *The Sufi Message of Hazrat Inayat Khan* (12 vols.). London: Barrie & Jenkins, 1970.*

Khan, Pir Vilayat. *Sufi Masters*. Paris and New York: Sufi Order, 1971.*

————. *Toward the One*. New York: Harper & Row, 1974.

Krishnabai, Mother. *Guru's Grace: Autobiography of Mother Krishnabai*. Translated by Swami Ramdass. Kanhangad, India: Anandashram, 1964.*

Krishnamurti, J. *Think on These Things*. New York: Harper & Row, 1970.

Langer, Jiri. *Nine Gates*. Cambridge, England: James Clarke & Co., 1961.

Lawrence, Brother. *The Practice of the Presence of God*. Garden City, New York: Doubleday, 1977.

Levin, Meyer. *Classic Hassidic Tales*. New York: Viking Penguin, 1975.

Levine, Stephen. *A Gradual Awakening*. Garden City, New York: Anchor/Doubleday, 1978.

Milarepa. *The Life of Milarepa*. Translated by Lobsang P. Lhalungpa. New York: E. P. Dutton, 1977.

Lysebeth, Andre Van. *Yoga Self-Taught*. New York: Harper & Row, 1973.

McNamara, William. *Christian Mysticism: The Art of the Inner Way*. Rockport, Massachusetts: Element Books, 1991.

Mahasi Sayadaw. *Practical Insight Meditation*. Santa Cruz, California: Unity Press, 1972.*

Mascaro, Juan, trans. *The Bhagavad Gita*. New York: Viking Penguin, 1962.

Meher Baba. *Discourses* (3 vols.). Walnut Creek, California: Sufism Reoriented, 1967; also Myrtle Beach, South Carolina: Sheriar Press.*

Merton, Thomas. *The Asian Journal of Thomas Merton*. New York: New Directions, 1968.

### RECOMMENDED READING

————, trans. *The Wisdom of the Desert*. New York: New Directions, 1960.

Mindell, Arnold. *Working on Yourself Alone*. London and New York: Arkana, 1990.

Mukerji, A. P. *The Spiritual Instructions of Swami Muktananda*. Clearlake, California: Dawn Horse Press, 1974.*

Nachman of Breslov, Rebbe. *Advice*. Translated by Avraham Greenbaum. Jerusalem: Breslov Research Institute, 1983.

Osborne, Arthur, ed. *The Teachings of Ramana Maharshi*. New York: Samuel Weiser, 1962.

Paramahansa Yogananda. *Autobiography of a Yogi*. Los Angeles: Self Realization Fellowship, 1975.

Paramananda, Swami. *Secret of Right Activity*. Cohasset, Massachusetts: Vedanta Center, 1964.*

Peers, E. Allison. *The Autobiography of St. Teresa of Avila*. Garden City, New York: Doubleday, 1960.

Pennington, Basil. *Centering Prayer: Renewing an Ancient Christian Prayer Form*. New York: Doubleday, 1982.*

Prabhavananda, Swami, and Christopher Isherwood, trans. *How to Know God: The Yoga Aphorisms of Patanjali*. New York: Signet, 1969.

Ram Dass. *Be Here Now*. New York: Harmony Books, 1971.

————. *Grist for the Mill*. Berkeley: Celestial Arts, 1987.

————. *The Only Dance There Is*. Garden City, New York: Doubleday, 1974.

Ramana Maharshi. *The Spiritual Teaching of Ramana Maharshi*. Boulder and London: Shambhala, 1972.

Reps, Paul. *Zen Flesh, Zen Bones*. Garden City, New York: Doubleday, 1957.

Schachter, Zalman. *Fragments of a Future Scroll*. Germantown, Pennsylvania: Leaves of Grass Press, 1975.*

Schimmel, Annemarie. *Mystical Dimensions of Islam*. Chapel Hill: University of North Carolina Press, 1978.

Scholem, Gershom. *Major Trends in Jewish Mysticism*. New York: Schocken Books, 1946.

Sivananda, Swami. *Japa Yoga*. Himalyas, India: Divine Life Society, 1972.*

### RECOMMENDED READING

Steinsaltz, Adin. *Beggars and Prayers*. New York: Basic Books, 1979.

Suzuki, Shunryu. *Zen Mind, Beginner's Mind*. New York: Weatherhill, 1970.

Teresa of Avila, Saint. *The Interior Castle*. Translated by K. Kavanaugh and O. Rodriguez. New York: Paulist Press, 1979.

Theophane the Monk. *Tales of a Magic Monastery*. New York: Crossroad Publishing, 1987.

Underhill, Evelyn. *Mystics of the Church*. Cambridge, England: James Clarke & Co., 1925.

———. *Mysticism*. New York: E. P. Dutton, 1974.

Vivekananda, Swami. *Karma Yoga and Bhakti Yoga*. New York: Ramakrishna-Vivekananda Center, 1973.*

———. *Raja Yoga*. New York: Ramakrishna-Vivekananda Center, 1955.*

Waddell, Helen. *The Desert Fathers*. Ann Arbor: University of Michigan Press, 1972.

Watts, Alan. *The Way of Zen*. New York: Pantheon Books, 1957.

Yogeshananda, Swami. *The Visions of Sri Ramakrishna*. Madras, India: Sri Ramakrishna Math, 1973.*

Yokoi, Yūhō, and Daizen Victoria. *Zen Master Dōgen*. New York: Weatherhill, 1976.

# INDEX

# ABOUT THE AUTHOR

David A. Cooper has been a student of mysticism for over thirty years. He is widely traveled and has extensively explored the mystical elements of a variety of traditions, including Buddhism, Christianity, Hinduism, Islam, and Judaism. He lived in the Old City of Jerusalem for eight years, studying the Hasidic and kabbalistic aspects of Judaism, culminating in his rabbinic ordination. In 1991 he and his wife, Shoshana, moved to the mountains of Colorado—near Boulder—where they caretake a modest, nondenominational retreat facility for individuals who wish to gain new awareness through the practice of silence and solitude. For information about retreats, please write to Heart of Stillness Retreats, P.O. Box 106, Jamestown, Colorado, 80435.

Noela N. Evans
MEDITATIONS FOR THE PASSAGES AND
CELEBRATIONS OF LIFE
*A Book of Vigils*
Articulating the unspoken emotions experienced at such times
as birth, death, and marriage.
0-517-59341-6 Hardcover


Burghild Nina Holzer
A WALK BETWEEN HEAVEN AND EARTH
*A Personal Journal on Writing and the Creative Process*
How keeping a journal focuses and expands our awareness of ourselves
and everything that touches our lives.
0-517-88096-2 Softcover


Greg Johanson and Ron Kurtz
GRACE UNFOLDING
*Psychotherapy in the Spirit of the Tao-te ching*
The interaction of client and therapist illuminated through the gentle
power and wisdom of Lao Tsu's ancient Chinese classic.
0-517-88130-6 Softcover


Selected by Marcia and Jack Kelly
ONE HUNDRED GRACES
A collection of mealtime blessings from many traditions, inscribed in
calligraphy reminiscent of the manuscripts of medieval Europe.
0-517-58567-7 Hardcover


Jack and Marcia Kelly
SANCTUARIES
*A Guide to Lodgings in Monasteries, Abbeys, and Retreats of the United States*
For those in search of renewal and a little peace; described by the *New
York Times* as "the *Michelin Guide* of the retreat set."
THE NORTHEAST 0-517-57727-5 Softcover
WEST COAST & SOUTHWEST 0-517-88007-5 Softcover


Barbara Lachman
THE JOURNAL OF HILDEGARD OF BINGEN
A year in the life of the 12th-century German saint—the diary she never
had the time to write herself.
0-517-59169-3 Hardcover


Gunilla Norris
BEING HOME
*A Book of Meditations*
An exquisite modern book of hours, a celebration of mindfulness in
everyday activities.
0-517-58159-0 Hardcover


Gunilla Norris
BECOMING BREAD
*Meditations on Loving and Transformation*
A book linking the food of the spirit—love—with the food
of the body—bread.
0-517-59168-5 Hardcover


Gunilla Norris
JOURNEYING IN PLACE
*Reflections from a Country Garden*
An examination of how we can experience the eternal wherever
we look in nature.
0-517-59762-4 Hardcover